Confiscation and Money Launderin

Law and Practice

A Guide for Enforcement Authorities

HOME OFFICE

Organised and International Crime Directorate

1997

LONDON: THE STATIONERY OFFICE

ISBN 0 11 341138 3

Printed in the United Kindom for The Stationery Office
Dd. 303453, 1/97, C30, 3396/4 5673, 364352

Contents

1
Preface

1.1   Powers to confiscate the proceeds of crime and to combat money laundering are a recent development in United Kingdom law but an extremely important one.

1.2   Since the entry into force of the Drug Trafficking Offences Act 1986 there has been intense legislative activity in this area. The 1986 Act has itself been amended on several occasions and has been consolidated in the Drug Trafficking Act 1994. New powers have been created to confiscate the proceeds of crimes other than drug trafficking, and terrorist funds, and Scotland and Northern Ireland have developed their own confiscation schemes.

1.3   With so much legislation in such a short space of time it would be surprising if more than a few practitioners were fully aware of everything that can be done, domestically and internationally, to confiscate the proceeds of crime. An overview of the whole field, taking in confiscation, money laundering and international co-operation, is much needed.

1.4   The main purpose of this guide is to provide a practical explanation of the legislation. Although the intention has been to be as accurate as possible, the guide should not be taken to be either a statement of the law or to reflect the official view of the Home Office on the legislation. Consequently no liability can be accepted for any unintended inaccuracy. It is hoped, however, that this guide will prove a useful introduction to the subject for law enforcement authorities and that it will encourage the fullest and most effective use of confiscation as a key weapon against serious crime.

PART 1
DOMESTIC LAW
AND PRACTICE

SECTION 1
INTRODUCTION TO DOMESTIC LAW

2

Introduction to domestic law

Drugs

2.1   Part 1 of the guide provides information about the domestic operation of the United Kingdom's confiscation statutes. For economy of space, it describes the drug trafficking provisions in full in Section 2. Section 3 then compares the scheme relating to other crimes with the drug trafficking provisions.

2.2   The United Kingdom comprises the three separate jurisdictions of England and Wales, Scotland, and Northern Ireland. Each possesses its own confiscation legislation. The Crown Dependencies of Jersey, Guernsey and the Isle of Man are not part of the United Kingdom and are not included in this guide. They have their own confiscation legislation.

2.3   A confiscation order under the law of all three constituent jurisdictions of the United Kingdom is **an order to pay a sum of money, expressed in sterling. It is not an order transferring the title of property**. A confiscation order may normally **only be made following a criminal conviction**.

2.4   The Drug Trafficking Offences Act 1986 was the first confiscation law enacted in England and Wales and formed the basis of subsequent confiscation legislation throughout the United Kingdom. Restricted, as the title of the Act suggests, to the confiscation of the proceeds of drug trafficking, its confiscation provisions came into force on 12 January 1987.

2.5   The Drug Trafficking Offences Act 1986 was amended by the Criminal Justice (Scotland) Act 1987, the Prevention of Terrorism (Temporary Provisions) Act 1989, the Criminal Justice (International Co-operation) Act 1990 and other legislation. To simplify and clarify the drug trafficking confiscation legislation, the 1986 Act was consolidated in the Drug Trafficking Act 1994, which came into force on 3 February 1995.

2.6   The confiscation provisions of the Drug Trafficking Act 1994 apply where a person is charged with one or more drug trafficking offences on or after commencement of the Act on 3 February 1995. The Drug Trafficking Offences Act 1986 as amended up to, **but not including**, the amendments to it contained in the Criminal Justice Act 1993, still applies where a person was charged with one or more drug trafficking offences before 3 February 1995.

2.7   Confiscation orders made under the Drug Trafficking Offences Act 1986 are enforced under that Act, not under the Drug Trafficking Act 1994. Consequently, it will be some time before all the "old" cases under the Drug Trafficking Offences Act 1986 have worked their way through the system. This guide looks to the future and describes the drug trafficking confiscation law of England and Wales as expressed in the Drug Trafficking Act 1994.

Other crime

2.8   Drug trafficking confiscation law has developed separately in the United Kingdom from the confiscation scheme relating to crime generally. Part VI of the Criminal Justice Act 1988 introduced for England and Wales powers to confiscate the proceeds of indictable offences generally (ie indictable offences other than drug trafficking offences - certain terrorist offences under Part III of the Prevention of Terrorism (Temporary Provisions) Act 1989 are now also excluded from the 1988 Act scheme). The 1988 Act also created the power to confiscate the proceeds of certain lucrative summary offences.

2.9   The confiscation scheme originally contained in Part VI of the Criminal Justice Act 1988 was much less robust, in several fundamental ways, from that created for drug trafficking by the Drug Trafficking Offences Act 1986. Part VI of the Criminal Justice Act 1988 has, however, been substantially amended by the Proceeds of Crime Act 1995 and has been brought more closely into line with the drug trafficking confiscation law in England and Wales.

2.10   Specific powers to enable a court, following conviction, to order the forfeiture of funds used, or intended for use, to finance terrorist groups or their activities were introduced in the Prevention of Terrorism (Temporary Provisions) Act 1989. These forfeiture powers apply throughout the United Kingdom.

Scotland

2.11   In Scotland, drug trafficking confiscation was first introduced in the Criminal Justice (Scotland) Act 1987. Scottish all crime confiscation legislation was brought forward in the Criminal Justice (Scotland) Act 1995 which also strengthened Scottish law on the forfeiture of instrumentalities. All of Scotland's confiscation legislation was subsequently consolidated in the Proceeds of Crime (Scotland) Act 1995, which entered into force on 1 April 1996 and implemented the all crime confiscation scheme enacted in the Criminal Justice (Scotland) Act 1995.

Northern Ireland

2.12   Northern Ireland has recently enacted the Proceeds of Crime (Northern Ireland) Order 1996 which replaces the Criminal Justice (Confiscation) (Northern Ireland) Order 1990. The 1996 Order provides for the confiscation by the Northern Irish courts of the proceeds of both drug trafficking and other serious crime. The 1996 Order reflects changes in the law of England and Wales up to and including the Drug Trafficking Act 1994 and the Proceeds of Crime Act 1995.

2.13   A range of secondary legislation has been made under powers contained in the primary legislation mentioned above, notably Orders in Council enabling the enforcement in the United Kingdom of confiscation and forfeiture orders made in other jurisdictions. These Orders in Council are described in Part 2 of the guide.

SECTION 2
DRUG TRAFFICKING CONFISCATION IN ENGLAND AND WALES

3

Investigations into drug trafficking

3.1   The Drug Trafficking Act 1994 contains strong powers to trace the proceeds of drug trafficking. These include the drug trafficking production order and search warrant.

3.2   The legislation allows drug trafficking investigations (including investigations into the financial aspects of drug trafficking) to be carried out without alerting the suspect. For example, application for a drug trafficking production order may be made to a Circuit judge *ex parte* (ie with nobody but the police or Customs and the judge involved). Furthermore, where a production order under the Act has been made or applied for and not refused, it is an offence to disclose information or any other matter that is likely to prejudice the investigation.

The production order

3.3   Section 55 of the Drug Trafficking Act contains the production order powers. It enables the police and Customs to obtain ordinary and "special procedure" material, that is to say banking and other confidential material, for the purpose of an investigation into drug trafficking. Application for a production order is made to a Circuit judge. Either police or Customs may apply. There is no need to inform the person who will be required to produce the material of the application before it is made.

3.4   Where there are reasonable grounds for suspecting that a specified person has carried on or benefited from drug trafficking, a Circuit judge may issue a production order requiring particular material, or material of a particular description, to be produced.

3.5   Many police officers will be familiar with Schedule 1 to the Police and Criminal Evidence Act 1984 ("PACE") which provides a useful point of comparison with the powers at section 55 of the Drug Trafficking Act. Schedule 1 to PACE permits the production of "special procedure material", which includes confidential banking material, for the purpose of an investigation into a serious arrestable offence and can be used to obtain material in connection with an investigation into a drug trafficking offence.

3.6   Under Schedule 1 to PACE, however, a production order will only be made where there are reasonable grounds for suspecting that a serious arrestable *offence* has taken place. Under section 55 of the Drug Trafficking Act, it is only necessary for there to be reasonable grounds for suspecting that a specified person has carried on, or has benefited from, drug trafficking. Consequently, a section 55 production order may be obtained at an earlier stage of the investigation than under Schedule 1 to PACE. It is not necessary to show that there are reasonable grounds to suspect that a specific offence has been committed.

3.7   Before granting a production order under section 55 of the Drug Trafficking Act the Circuit judge must be satisfied that:

- a specified person has carried on or has benefited from drug trafficking;

- the material to be produced is likely to be of substantial value to the drug trafficking investigation for the purpose of which the application is made;

- the material does not include items subject to legal privilege or "excluded material"; and

- there are reasonable grounds for believing that it is in the public interest for the material to be made available, having regard to the benefit likely to accrue to the investigation and the circumstances under which the person possessing the material holds it.

3.8   The terms "subject to legal privilege" and "excluded material" have the same meaning as in PACE. "Items subject to legal privilege" are defined in section 10 of PACE and, broadly, are communications between a professional legal adviser and the adviser's client about legal advice or legal proceedings, together with items included in or referred to in such communications, provided that the items are not being held with the intention of furthering a criminal purpose.

3.9   "Excluded material" is defined in section 11 of PACE. It includes personal records compiled in the course of a business, human tissue held for diagnosis or treatment, and journalistic material, provided these items are held in confidence.

3.10   A section 55 production order is an order for the production of particular material or material of a particular description, so the material to be produced must be identified in the application for the order. The material must also be in existence at the time of applying for the order. It is not possible to obtain a production order prospectively, that is to say for material which might come into existence after the order has been made.

3.11   A section 55 production order may require any person in possession of material likely to be of substantial value to an investigation, including government departments, to produce material to the enforcement authorities; and a section 55 production order overrides any obligation as to secrecy or any other restriction upon the disclosure of information imposed by statute or otherwise.

3.12   Where the Circuit judge is satisfied that the necessary conditions are met, a production order will be made requiring the person who appears to be in possession of the material to produce it to a police or Customs officer to take away. Or the order may require the person in possession of the material to give a police or Customs officer access to it.

3.13   If the information is held on computer, as it often will be where the contents of bank accounts and similar financial material are concerned, it must be produced in a visible and legible form. The Circuit judge may also order any person who appears to be able to grant access to the premises on which the material is held to allow the police or Customs officer to enter.

3.14   The time allowed for compliance with the order will normally be 7 days, but the Circuit judge may specify a longer or shorter period if it seems appropriate in a particular case. Any person required to comply with a section 55 production order may apply, in accordance with Rules of Court, for the discharge or variation of the order.

3.15   The Rule of Court applicable to the discharge and variation of production orders under section 55 of the Drug Trafficking Act is Rule 25B of the Crown Court Rules 1982 which was made in the Crown Court (Amendment) Rules 1986 (SI 1986/2151(L.17)). It sets out the procedure governing applications for variation or discharge of an order. It explains that on hearing an application for the discharge or variation of an order a Circuit judge may discharge the order or make such variations to it as he or she thinks fit.

Search and seizure

3.16   Section 56 of the Drug Trafficking Act 1994 enables a police or Customs officer to apply to a Circuit judge for a warrant to search specified premises for the purpose of an investigation into drug trafficking.

3.17   As with the drug trafficking production order described above, police officers may note the similarities between these powers and the earlier provisions of Schedule 1 to PACE relating to search for and seizure of special procedure material.

3.18   Like a section 55 production order, a warrant under section 56 of the Drug Trafficking Act may be granted by a Circuit judge without the police or Customs needing to demonstrate reasonable grounds for suspecting that a specific offence has taken place. A section 56 warrant may be issued where any of three sets of conditions is satisfied.

3.19   The first is that a production order has been made under section 55 of the Drug Trafficking Act but has not been complied with. The second is that all the conditions for making a section 55 production order are satisfied but it would be inappropriate to make one because either:

- it is not practicable to communicate with any person entitled to produce the material or to grant access to the material or the premises where it is held; or

- the investigation might be seriously prejudiced without immediate access to the material in question.

3.20   The third is that there are reasonable grounds for suspecting that a specified person has carried on or has benefited from drug trafficking, and that:

- the premises contain material relating to the specified person or to drug trafficking which is likely to be of substantial value to the investigation, but the material cannot be particularised at the time of the application; and

- it is not practicable to communicate with any person entitled to grant access to the premises; or entry will not be granted unless a warrant is produced; or the investigation might be seriously prejudiced without immediate entry to the premises.

3.21   Where a Circuit judge has issued a section 56 warrant, the police or Customs may seize from the premises any material other than excluded material or items subject to legal privilege which is likely to be of substantial value to the investigation for the purpose of which the warrant was issued. "Excluded material" and "items subject to legal privilege" have the meaning attributed to them by PACE, as described in paragraphs 3.8 and 3.9 above.

3.22   Where a section 56 warrant has been issued, it is an offence under section 58 of the Drug Trafficking Act to make any disclosure likely to prejudice the investigation. This offence is intended to deter "tipping off".

Asset tracing assistance to other jurisdictions

3.23   The Drug Trafficking Act defines drug trafficking as doing or being concerned in any one or more of a number of illegal drug related activities, *whether in England and Wales or elsewhere*. The section 55 and 56 powers are available for the purpose of an investigation into drug trafficking. Consequently, the police and Customs can use the powers to have banking and similar material produced in England and Wales on behalf of investigations into drug trafficking which are being carried on abroad.

3.24   Assistance of this nature may be provided by the police and Customs without any need for a treaty or agreement with the foreign country concerned. Part 2 of the guide contains further information about assistance to other jurisdictions in tracing, freezing and confiscating the proceeds of drug trafficking.

Financial Investigators

3.25   The National Criminal Intelligence Service holds details of United Kingdom Financial Investigators (primarily Financial Investigators working in police forces, Regional Crime Squads and HM Customs and Excise). It also holds details of Money Laundering Reporting Officers working in financial institutions (see paragraph 17.6 below). These schedules are regularly updated and forwarded annually to all banks and forces.

4
The preservation of assets

The restraint order

4.1   Powers to prevent dealing in property in advance of and during criminal proceedings are essential. Otherwise it may be hidden, dissipated or removed from the jurisdiction. These powers are referred to in the Drug Trafficking Act, and in United Kingdom confiscation law generally, as **restraint**. Property itself is not restrained; rather, a person is "restrained", by order of the court, from dealing with it.

4.2   The Drug Trafficking Act allows restraint action to be taken in advance of and during the proceedings to ensure that assets are available to satisfy any confiscation order that may be, or has been, made. The main features of the provisions are:

●   application for a restraint order must be made by the prosecutor;

●   application must be made to the High Court;

●   application may be made *ex parte* to a judge "in chambers" (ie. in court, but in closed session) so that the defendant does not find out about the restraint order until it has been made; and

●   proceedings must have been instituted, or the High Court must be satisfied that they are about to be, or the prosecutor must have applied, or be about to apply, for a revaluation of the defendant's proceeds of drug trafficking. (Revaluation is described in Chapter 8.)

4.3   The restraint powers are contained in sections 25 and 26 of the Drug Trafficking Act. The proceedings in the High Court are civil, not criminal. The procedure involved in applying to the High Court for a restraint order is set out in Order 115 of the Rules of the Supreme Court. It is not necessary, when applying for a restraint order, to establish that any property which may be mentioned in the order is the proceeds of drug trafficking. It is, however, necessary for the court to be satisfied that there is reasonable cause to believe that the defendant has benefited from drug trafficking.

4.4   A restraint order can be obtained to prevent anybody at all from dealing in any "realisable" property (ie any property held by the defendant or by a person to whom the defendant has made a gift caught by the Act). Practitioners should be aware that the value of certain gifts made by the defendant to other people is confiscable, and that restraint can be used to help ensure that the value of a gift can be recovered from its recipient (further information on gifts is contained in paragraph 5.35).

4.5   In most cases, the restraint order will be made against the defendant, or a partner. In making a restraint order the High Court may specify conditions and exceptions. For example, it may allow dealing in property for reasonable living or legal expenses. What constitutes a reasonable living expense may vary from one defendant to another.

4.6　　　Under the Rules of the Supreme Court, Order 115, the prosecutor must serve a copy of the restraint order, and the affidavit produced when it was applied for, on every named person restrained by the order, and must notify everybody else affected by the order of its terms.

4.7　　　Where, for example, a restraint order is made against a defendant who controls money in a certain bank account, the defendant will be served with the order and restrained from dealing in the money by the order. The bank will be notified of the order because it is affected by the order's terms. It is required not to contravene the order by permitting dealing with the money in the account. Anybody contravening a restraint order is liable to proceedings for contempt of court.

4.8　　　The Drug Trafficking Act contains a number of ancillary provisions to ensure that the restraint powers work effectively. Once a restraint order has been made, the High Court and a county court may appoint a receiver to take possession of, manage or deal with any realisable property. They may also order anybody holding such property to hand it over to the receiver.

4.9　　　This provision makes it possible for property to be liquidated at an early stage in the proceedings. It may be desirable to do so occasionally even before the conviction on which the confiscation order depends has been obtained and before any appeal against the conviction has been disposed of, particularly where a property is in danger of falling into serious disrepair.

4.10　　　In addition, section 26(9) of the Drug Trafficking Act allows a police or Customs officer to seize any property subject to a restraint order for the purpose of preventing its removal from Great Britain. The use of this provision is particularly appropriate where there are grounds to suspect that an attempt to remove a valuable asset, for example a yacht, is being planned.

The charging order

4.11　　　Where the defendant, or a person to whom the defendant has made a gift caught by the Act, holds property in the form of land or certain kinds of securities such as government stock or units of a unit trust, it may be convenient to apply to the High Court for a charging order, rather than a restraint order, in respect of the property.

4.12　　　Like a restraint order, a charging order may be made both in advance of and during the proceedings. Whereas a restraint order is an order preventing a person from dealing in property, a charging order is made against the property itself.

4.13　　　A charging order under the Drug Trafficking Act secures payment of all or part of the value of the property charged to the Crown. Where a confiscation order has not yet been made, the charging order will secure the value of the property charged to the Crown. Where a confiscation order has been made, only the payment of an amount not exceeding the value of the confiscation order may be secured. The law recognises that it would not be right to allow a charging order to be made for a sum higher than the value of the confiscation order, once it has been made.

4.14　　　Sections 25, 27 and 28 of the Drug Trafficking Act contain the charging order provisions. As with restraint orders, application for a charging order must be made to the High Court by the prosecutor, may only be made when proceedings have been, or are about to be instituted, or where the prosecutor has made, or is about to make an application for revaluation, and may be made *ex parte* to a judge in chambers.

4.15　　　The procedure governing charging order applications is set out in Order 115 of the Rules of the Supreme Court. Once a charging order has been made, the prosecutor must serve a copy of the order and the affidavit in support on the defendant and, in certain cases, on others.

4.16   In the case of securities the charge may extend to any interest or dividend payable in respect of the asset. A charging order may be made either absolutely or subject to conditions. Like restraint orders, charging orders may be discharged or varied by the High Court after they have been made, and they must be discharged if the sum they are designed to secure payment of to the Crown is paid into court.

Disclosure of information held by government departments

4.17   Section 59 of the Drug Trafficking Act provides powers for the High Court to order the disclosure of information held by government departments for the purpose of facilitating the restraint, charging or realisation of property under the Act.

4.18   An application for an order for the disclosure of material held by a government department must be made by the prosecutor to the High Court. It may be made at any time between the institution and conclusion of proceedings, or before proceedings are instituted if the High Court has already made a restraint or charging order in the case.

4.19   A section 59 order to produce material to the High Court (or to disclose it further) overrides any obligation of secrecy or any other restriction on the disclosure of information imposed by statute on the government department. The order will normally be served on the department's solicitor, but obliges any officer of the department who may be in possession of the material to comply with the terms of the order.

4.20   A section 59 order will require the government department in question to produce to the High Court, within whatever period the court specifies, all or part of the material in its possession which relates to the defendant or to another person who has at any time held property which was realisable property. Such material may include documents which originated from the defendant, or from such a person; documents prepared by the department's officials; or correspondence.

4.21   The High Court may order that all or part of the material disclosed by a government department under section 59 of the Drug Trafficking Act is to be disclosed to a receiver appointed in the case, to assist the receiver in the restraint and realisation of property, or in pursuance of a charging order, but only after the government department in question has had a reasonable opportunity to make representations to the court.

4.22   Subject to any conditions imposed by the order, the receiver may then disclose the information further for the purposes of any of the receiver's own functions under the Drug Trafficking Act, or the functions of the Crown Court under the Act.

4.23   Those functions do not include the functions of either the receiver or the Crown Court under section 16 of the Drug Trafficking Act ("Increase in realisable property"), which was formerly section 16 of the Criminal Justice (International Co-operation) Act 1990.

4.24   The High Court may also order the disclosure of any of the material produced by a government department under section 59 of the Drug Trafficking Act to a police or Customs officer, or to a member of the Crown Prosecution Service. The government department in question must first have been given a reasonable opportunity to make representations to the court. The material must also be likely to be of substantial value in exercising functions relating to drug trafficking. Such material may then be further disclosed, subject to any restrictions imposed by the court, for the purposes of functions relating to drug trafficking.

Delay in notifying arrest

4.25   Another provision to help prevent the dissipation of assets is contained in the sections of PACE which deal with the rights of arrested persons to have someone informed of their arrest, and to have access to legal advice.

4.26   PACE specifies the circumstances in which the exercise of those rights may be delayed. Delay may be authorised where the authorising officer has reasonable grounds for believing that the detained person has benefited from drug trafficking, and that the exercise of the rights would hinder the recovery of the value of that person's proceeds of drug trafficking.

4.27   Delay may only be authorised by a police officer of superintendent rank or above, or a Customs officer within job band 9 or above, and may be for a maximum of 36 hours. The provision is intended to allow a restraint or charging order to be sought before the detained person's associates hear of the arrest.

Bankruptcy, insolvency and liquidation

4.28   The situation may sometimes arise where the defendant is subject to both confiscation and insolvency proceedings. Sections 32 to 36 of the Drug Trafficking Act contain extensive provision to deal with this situation. A detailed analysis is beyond the scope of this guide, but it is important that practitioners should be aware of the basic features of the legislation and the principles underlying them.

4.29   The purpose of the insolvency provisions in the Drug Trafficking Act is to take account of the needs of genuine creditors whilst at the same time ensuring that drug traffickers are given no opportunity to engineer the proceeds of drug trafficking into the hands of others by means of contrived insolvency proceedings.

4.30   Consequently, the restraint, charging and realisation powers available under the Drug Trafficking Act may not be exercised in respect of property which forms part of a bankrupt's estate or is subject to the functions of a liquidator, where a bankruptcy order, winding-up order or resolution for voluntary winding-up is already in force at the time of the application for the exercise of the powers under the Drug Trafficking Act.

4.31   Where, on the other hand, a restraint or charging order has already been made in respect of property, or the property has already been realised under the Drug Trafficking Act at the time of the order adjudging a person bankrupt, the winding up order, or the resolution for voluntary winding up, the property is excluded from the bankrupt's estate, and from the functions of the liquidator or provisional liquidator in the case of a company, until proceedings under the Drug Trafficking Act have been concluded.

4.32   Where property is not subject to restraint, charging or realisation because it is already the subject of a bankruptcy order, winding up order or resolution for voluntary winding up, the Crown Court should still take it into account in assessing the value of the defendant's proceeds of drug trafficking and setting the amount of the confiscation order.

4.33   This allows the value of any property not ultimately required to satisfy creditors to be confiscated. The shortfall in meeting the full amount of the confiscation order as a result of satisfying the creditors can be dealt with by an application to the High Court by or on behalf of the defendant for a downward variation of the confiscation order under section 17 of the Drug Trafficking Act (see Chapter 8 for a description of those procedures).

5

The drug trafficking confiscation order

5.1   **A confiscation order under the confiscation legislation of England and Wales is an order to pay a sum of money, expressed in sterling. It is not an order transferring the title of property.** The purpose of a confiscation order under the Drug Trafficking Act is to deprive the drug trafficker of the value of his or her proceeds of drug trafficking. Once triggered, the confiscation procedures are mandatory and the court has no discretion as to the amount of the confiscation order. There is no question of an accommodation between the prosecution and the defence as to the amount of a confiscation order.

5.2   The High Court has the power to make a confiscation order against a drug trafficker who dies after conviction but before a confiscation order could be made in the Crown Court, and against a person convicted of or charged with one or more drug trafficking offences who then absconds. These procedures are described in Chapter 7.

5.3   In all other cases, a drug trafficking confiscation order will be made in the Crown Court following a person's appearance before the court for sentence after having been convicted of one or more drug trafficking offence as defined in section 1 of the Drug Trafficking Act. The list of drug trafficking offences found in that section comprises the full range of offences involving controlled drugs, including drug money laundering offences, but excluding simple possession. Because the confiscation order (with the exception of one made against an absconder) depends on a conviction, if the conviction is quashed, any confiscation order dependent on it must fall too.

5.4   The confiscation procedures in the Drug Trafficking Act are not to be triggered where the person appearing for sentence before the Crown Court has been committed to the Crown Court under section 37(1) of the Magistrates' Courts Act 1980 (committal with a view to sentence of detention in a young offender institution) or if the powers of the Crown Court are limited to dealing with the defendant in a way that a magistrates' court might have dealt with the defendant. An example of the latter would be the case where a juvenile is tried at the Crown Court solely by virtue of having been charged jointly with an adult.

Sequence of the confiscation procedures

5.5   Where a person has been convicted of a drug trafficking offence in proceedings instituted on or after 3 February 1995 and appears before the Crown Court for sentence, the prosecutor may ask the Crown Court to proceed under section 2 of the Drug Trafficking Act, ie. to go through the mandatory confiscation procedures set out in section 2 of the Act. If the court is asked to proceed, it must do so. Alternatively, the prosecutor may decide not to ask the court to proceed, but the court may still elect to proceed of its own accord.

Postponement

5.6   Whether the prosecutor triggers the confiscation procedures or the court proceeds of its own accord, the court will need to decide the order in which sentence and the making of a confiscation order should take place.

5.7   The court may wish to sentence the defendant first and consider the confiscation matters subsequently. Section 3 of the Drug Trafficking Act makes this possible. The court's power to postpone the confiscation matters is available in all cases to which the Act applies, that is to say where the defendant has been charged on or after 3 February 1995 with the drug trafficking offence(s) which have led to the conviction in respect of which the confiscation procedures have been triggered.

5.8   Under section 3 of the Drug Trafficking Act, where the Crown Court considers that it requires further information before determining whether the defendant has benefited from drug trafficking, or the amount to be recovered under the confiscation order, it may postpone making either determination for such period as it may specify, and proceed to sentence the defendant immediately or at any time during the period of postponement. If it postpones determination, it must not include a fine, forfeiture or deprivation order in sentencing. These can, however, be imposed later.

5.9   More than one postponement can be made, but the total period of postponement must not exceed six months from the date of conviction, unless the court is satisfied that there are exceptional circumstances. Where the defendant appeals against conviction, the court may still postpone the determinations mentioned in paragraph 5.8 but the period of postponement cannot exceed three months from the date of the determination of the appeal, unless the court is satisfied that there are exceptional circumstances.

5.10   Further provisions covering the situation where postponement is affected by an appeal against conviction are set out in the Crown Court (Amendment) (No.2) Rules 1994 [S.I. 1994/3153 (L.19)].

5.11   Under the postponement provisions, therefore, where the confiscation procedures are triggered the Crown Court can:

   (a)   postpone, then sentence immediately, then consider confiscation in the period of postponement; or

   (b)   postpone, then consider confiscation, then sentence at any time in the period of postponement.

5.12   **It should be noted that, as a consequence of these provisions, in any case where the confiscation procedures are triggered and the Crown Court wishes to sentence the defendant before resolving the confiscation issues it should first postpone under section 3 of the Drug Trafficking Act before sentencing.**

5.13   Where the prosecutor, following a conviction, triggers the confiscation procedures, it will be appropriate for the prosecutor to consider whether the court will need to postpone and, if so, to suggest to the court at the same time that it postpones confiscation.

5.14   The prosecutor may also use this occasion to serve a statement on the defendant under section 11(5) of the Drug Trafficking Act setting out the defendant's benefit from drug trafficking (the "section 11 statement" is described below). When specifying the first period of postponement, the Crown Court may wish also to nominate a period within which the defendant must respond to the prosecutor's statement.

Determining whether the defendant has benefited from drug trafficking

5.15   Under the Drug Trafficking Act, once the prosecutor has triggered the confiscation procedures the Crown Court must first decide whether the convicted defendant has benefited from drug trafficking. For the purposes of the Act, a person has benefited from drug trafficking if he or she has received any payment or reward in connection with drug trafficking carried on by him/her, or by another person, at any time. Drug trafficking means drug trafficking carried on **anywhere in the world**.

5.16   The standard of proof applicable in determining any question under the Drug Trafficking Act as to whether the defendant has benefited from drug trafficking, and the amount to be recovered under the confiscation order, is the civil standard (the balance of probabilities) (see section 2(8) of the Act).

Determining the value of the proceeds

5.17   If the court determines that the defendant has benefited from drug trafficking it must then work out by how much (the value of the defendant's proceeds of drug trafficking) and, unless the question of the amount that might be realised is raised, it must then order the defendant to pay that amount. That is the confiscation order.

5.18   It will be noted that the basic confiscation procedures only require the court to ask itself two questions:

- has the defendant benefited from drug trafficking?

- if so, what is the value of the defendant's proceeds of drug trafficking?

The assumptions

5.19   To overcome the difficulties inherent in determining whether the defendant has benefited from drug trafficking, and establishing which parts of the defendant's present wealth represent the proceeds of past drug trafficking, the Drug Trafficking Act requires the court to make certain assumptions about the illicit origins of the defendant's property.

5.20   With the exceptions described in paragraphs 5.22 and 5.23 below, the Crown Court must make the assumptions in all cases where the confiscation procedures are triggered. The assumptions are that any property appearing to the court:

- to have been held by the defendant at any time since conviction; or

- to have been transferred to the defendant in the 6 years before the institution of the present proceedings

was received by the defendant from his or her drug trafficking.

5.21   It must also be assumed:

- that any expenditure of the defendant's in the six years ending with the institution of proceedings was made out of payments received from his or her drug trafficking; and

- that for the purpose of valuing any property received or assumed to have been received by the defendant out of the defendant's drug trafficking, it was received free of any other interests in it.

5.22   The assumptions cannot be made if the only drug trafficking offences in respect of which the defendant appears before the court for sentence are drug money laundering offences.

5.23   Furthermore, an assumption will not be made if it is shown to be incorrect in the defendant's case. The court may also decide, exceptionally, not to make any one or more of the required assumptions if it is satisfied that there would be a serious risk of injustice in the defendant's case if the assumption were made. Where the court does not make one or more of the assumptions for either of the reasons mentioned in this paragraph, however, it must state its reasons for not doing so.

5.24   The effect of the assumptions is to cut through any steps taken by the defendant to disguise the illegal origin of his/her property. The Act starts from the premise that all the defendant's property was obtained illegally, and then requires the defendant to demonstrate which of it, if any, was received legitimately.

Statements relating to drug trafficking

5.25   The court will obviously find it helpful, in determining whether the defendant has benefited from drug trafficking and determining the value of the defendant's proceeds, to have before it information about the defendant's financial dealings. Section 11 of the Drug Trafficking Act provides for such information to be put before the court by the prosecutor in the form of a statement.

5.26   Section 11 should be read in conjunction with Rule 25A of the Crown Court Rules 1982, as amended by the Crown Court (Amendment) Rules 1995 [S.I. 1995/2618(L.9)]. Amongst other things, the Rules of Court specify what particulars must be put in the statement.

5.27   Section 11 of the Drug Trafficking Act requires the prosecutor to produce a statement to the court *in every case* where the prosecutor triggers the confiscation procedures. The statement will enable the prosecutor to bring to the court's attention any relevant information about the defendant's financial dealings gathered by the enforcement authorities during the investigation, and any information obtained by a receiver already appointed in connection with a restraint order.

5.28   Section 11 also empowers the court to require of the prosecutor as many further statements as it thinks fit, and to require of the prosecutor a statement or statements where it proceeds of its own volition. Section 11 leaves it up to the court to decide how long to give the prosecutor to produce a statement, and how long to allow the defendant to respond to it. The amount of time allowed will vary case by case.

Order to defendant to provide information

5.29   For the purpose of obtaining information to assist it in carrying out its functions, the Crown Court may at any time order the defendant under section 12 of the Drug Trafficking Act to give it such information as may be specified in the order, in such manner and by such date as may also be specified in the order.

5.30   If the defendant fails, without reasonable excuse, to comply with the order, the court is free to draw such inferences from that failure as it considers appropriate. Where, however, the prosecutor accepts to any extent an allegation made by the defendant in response to such an order, the court may treat the prosecutor's acceptance as conclusive of the matters to which it relates.

The amount that might be realised

5.31   One of the fundamental principles of confiscation is that the amount which the defendant is ordered to pay and which is to be recovered under a confiscation order should be no more than the value of the property which is available for confiscation. Consequently, the Drug Trafficking Act provides that where the amount that is confiscable is lower than the value of the defendant's proceeds, the defendant shall only be ordered to pay an order whose value is equal to the amount confiscable.

5.32   The court need only enquire into the amount actually confiscable, referred to in the Act as "the amount that might be realised", if asked to do so by the defendant. Furthermore, the burden of proving that the amount that might be realised is lower than the value of the proceeds (and hence, that a smaller confiscation order should be imposed) rests on the defendant.

5.33   If the amount that might be realised turns out to be greater than or equal to the total value of the defendant's proceeds of drug trafficking, the court must make a confiscation order in the full value of the defendant's proceeds of drug trafficking. If the amount that might be realised is less than the total value of the defendant's proceeds of drug trafficking, the court must make a confiscation order for the amount that might be realised.

5.34   **To sum up, the amount which the defendant is ordered to pay and which is to be recovered under a confiscation order will be the total amount of the defendant's proceeds unless the defendant raises the question of the amount that might be realised and can prove that the amount that might be realised is lower than the total amount of his/her proceeds.**

5.35   The amount that might be realised is defined by the Act as the total value of the realisable property held by the defendant, minus the total amounts of any obligations having priority, plus the value of any gifts caught by the Act. A gift is "caught" by the Drug Trafficking Act if it was made by the defendant in the six years before the institution of proceedings, or was made at any time out of the proceeds of drug trafficking. For the purposes of the Act a gift includes any property transferred by the defendant for significantly less than its full value.

5.36   "Realisable property" is defined by the Act as any property held by the defendant and any property held by a person to whom the defendant has directly or indirectly made a gift caught by the Act. It is important to bear in mind that this means legally as well as illegally obtained property, and that a confiscation order can be enforced against both. The value of a gift caught by the Act may be realised from any property held by the recipient of the gift, but no more than the value of the gift may be realised from that property. Property is not realisable property if certain types of order, such as a forfeiture order, are already in force against it (ie. the order has been made in respect of it in **previous** proceedings).

5.37   Broadly speaking, "obligations having priority" over a confiscation order are the defendant's debts where the state is a secured creditor.

5.38   It will be noted that if the defendant raises the question of the amount that might be realised, the court will ask itself two further questions:

- what is the amount that might be realised in satisfaction of a confiscation order against the defendant?

- is the amount that might be realised higher or lower than the defendant's proceeds of drug trafficking?

5.39   The defendant may give the Crown Court a statement under section 11 of the Drug Trafficking Act concerning the amount that might be realised under any confiscation order made. The prosecutor's acceptance, to any extent, of any allegation in it may be treated by the court as conclusive of the matters to which it relates. Where the defendant tenders a statement under section 11 a copy of it must be sent to the prosecutor as soon as is practicable (see Rule 25A of the Crown Court Rules 1982 as amended by the Crown Court (Amendment) Rules 1995 [S.I. 1995/2618(L.9)]).

5.40   Where the court orders an amount to be paid under the confiscation order lower than the defendant's proceeds of drug trafficking, it must issue a certificate under section 5 of the Drug Trafficking Act setting out the basis of its determination. The court may also issue a certificate in other circumstances, setting out any points on which it is satisfied about the realisable property available and its value. These certificates are useful when it comes to enforcing the confiscation order.

Ancillary matters

5.41   Where the court makes a confiscation order, it must also set a term of imprisonment in default of payment and may allow time to pay and payment by instalments. The court has no power to order the satisfaction of a confiscation order out of specific items of property.

Confiscation orders in nominal amounts

5.42   Where the amount that might be realised is nil, the court should order the payment of a nominal amount. Justices' Clerks need take no steps to enforce such orders, if received for enforcement, and they should be treated for this purpose as if the amount specified in them were nil.

6

The enforcement of drug trafficking confiscation orders

General

6.1   Under the Drug Trafficking Act, Justices' Clerks are responsible for enforcing confiscation orders. This is because section 9(1) of the Act states that sections 31(1) to 3(C) and 32(1) and (2) of the Powers of Criminal Courts Act 1973 are to have effect as if the confiscation order were a Crown Court fine. Under the 1973 Act, Crown Court fines are enforced by the magistrates' court. The relevant fine enforcement provisions are contained in Part III of the Magistrates' Courts Act 1980. Justices' Clerks are responsible for enforcing both orders made by the Crown Court and those made by the High Court against dead or absconded drug traffickers.

6.2   The receipt by a Justices' Clerk of any sum in satisfaction of a confiscation order serves to reduce the amount payable under the order. The order is, of course, satisfied when no further amount remains payable. After making any deductions permitted by section 30 of the Drug Trafficking Act, Justices' Clerks must pay the residue of any sums they receive in satisfaction of a confiscation order to the Lord Chancellor, for transfer into the Consolidated Fund.

6.3   Monies must be deducted from the sums received in the strict order set out in section 30(5) to (8) of the Act, and applied, if necessary, to make the following payments:

- first, the expenses of an insolvency practitioner who has seized property subject to a restraint order, and which have not been paid already out of the gross sums in the hands of a receiver appointed under section 26 or 29 of the Act, or in pursuance of a charging order (see section 35(3));

- second, if the money was paid to the Justices' Clerk by such a receiver, the receiver's remuneration and expenses;

- third, the prosecutor, or some other person on whose application the receiver was appointed, must be reimbursed for any monies paid to the receiver at a time when there were no monies in the hands of the Justices' Clerk to pay the receiver as set out under the second head above.

It will be noted that only the second of these deductions will be made with any frequency, and that receivers' remuneration and expenses are paid out of the **gross** sums received by the Justices' Clerk.

6.4   Where the Crown Court makes a confiscation order it will specify by order a magistrates' court under section 32(1)(a) of the Powers of Criminal Courts Act 1973 to enforce the confiscation order. Where it does not specify an enforcing magistrates' court, the magistrates' court responsible for enforcement will be the one that committed the defendant to the Crown Court for trial. As soon as the Crown Court receives notice that the defendant wishes to appeal against an order, or against the conviction on which the order depends, the Crown Court will notify the enforcing magistrates' court so that enforcement is put on hold, pending the outcome of the appeal.

6.5 An important difference between confiscation order enforcement and fine enforcement is that magistrates' courts have no power to remit all or part of a confiscation order. The Crown Court or, as the case may be, the High Court should always have determined in advance that the amount of the order is pitched no higher than the amount that might be realised. That amount is determined not according to an assessment of continuing and future means, but to an assessment of the value of property available for realisation at the time the order is made, including, where appropriate, property held by third parties who have received a gift caught by the Act.

6.6 A confiscation order made in a nominal amount under section 5(3)(b) of the Drug Trafficking Act 1994 should be treated for accounting purposes as if it were an order to pay nil and should not be enforced. No nominal amount for such orders is specified in the legislation, but it is suggested that an appropriate sum is one penny, to avoid possible confusion with orders which may be made occasionally in small amounts, and which are required to be enforced.

6.7 The Crown Court, upon making a confiscation order, should send to the magistrates' court responsible for its enforcement copies of the order itself, the court record sheet, copies of any restraint or charging order in force, and any other material likely to assist in enforcement.

6.8 This should include, for example, any section 11 statements tendered to the Crown Court by either prosecutor or defendant, and any certificate issued by the Crown Court under section 5 of the Act (court's opinion on any matters relating to the amount that might be realised in satisfaction of a confiscation order).

6.9 It is also vital that the enforcing magistrates' court has all the available information on the whereabouts of the realisable property, and the address of both the defendant and the defendant's solicitor. The material should include the name and station of any police officer holding any money.

Application of fine enforcement powers

6.10 Because a confiscation order is treated in many respects as a fine, the Crown Court may allow time to pay and payment by instalments. Where time to pay is not allowed, payment is due forthwith. It is also important to note that enforcement of a confiscation order by means of the appointment of a receiver may commence immediately the order has been made and any appeal has been disposed of, regardless of any time to pay allowed. This means of confiscation order enforcement is additional to normal fine enforcement procedures and is described in paragraph 6.19 below.

6.11 It may be appropriate to allow time to pay where it is clear to the Crown Court that the confiscation order cannot be settled immediately by the defendant because, for example, assets need to be sold. Where time to pay is allowed, a clear date should be specified for when payment is to fall due.

Distress warrants

6.12 Because Part III of the Magistrates' Courts Act 1980 applies to confiscation order enforcement, the Justices' Clerk of the enforcing magistrates' court may apply for a distress warrant to have the defendant's goods sold and the sums raised paid in satisfaction of the confiscation order. The procedures involved are described in Rule 54 of the Magistrates' Courts Rules 1981.

6.13 It sometimes occurs that the police and Customs seize cash from persons subsequently convicted of a drug trafficking offence, and the question of the application of the cash in satisfaction of the confiscation order arises. It should be stressed once again that a confiscation order is an order to pay an amount of money, not an order altering the title of property, and so the Crown Court has no power to order the payment of such cash to the Justices' Clerk in satisfaction of the confiscation order.

6.14   In the circumstances just described the cash still belongs to the defendant even after the confiscation order is made. The defendant may well be prepared to provide authority for the police or Customs to hand it over to the Justices' Clerk in satisfaction of the confiscation order. In other cases, the cash can be transferred to the Justices' Clerk by means of a distress warrant.

Garnishee orders

6.15   Where satisfaction of a confiscation order can be met by the payment into court of sums held on the defendant's behalf by a third party such as a bank or building society, it will often be appropriate for the magistrates' court to exercise the powers in section 87 of the Magistrates' Courts Act 1980 to take civil action in the county court or, depending on the sums involved, the High Court.

6.16   Money deposited in a bank is a debt owed by the bank to the depositor. A garnishee order is an order requiring the bank (or whoever) to pay the debt not to the creditor (the defendant) but to another party (in the case of confiscation orders, the Justices' Clerk). The enforcing magistrates' court need not hold a means enquiry nor give the clerk of the court authority before such action is taken.

6.17   Garnishee proceedings are likely to be a particularly effective part of enforcement in cases where sums are lodged in bank and building society accounts and there is a restraint order in force. If the restraint order, a copy of which should be among the papers sent from the Crown Court to the enforcing magistrates' court, does not appear to allow for sums to be released for the purposes of enforcement, the prosecutor responsible for the case should be asked to apply to the High Court for the necessary provision to be made.

6.18   The full procedures for obtaining a garnishee order in the county court are set out in Order 30 of the County Court Rules 1981 and at pages 380-388 of the County Court Practice 1996. The corresponding High Court procedures are in Order 49 of the Rules of the Supreme Court and at pages 785-802 of Volume 1 of the Supreme Court Practice 1995.

Enforcement involving receivers

6.19   Receivers play an important role in the enforcement of confiscation orders because of the large amounts of some orders, the need to realise property forcibly and the need to liquidate real estate owned jointly by the defendant and some other person, particularly a spouse. A receiver may well be appointed in a case involving a gift or gifts caught by the Act, as it is the receiver who has the power, on the order of the High Court, to realise property in the hands of the recipient of the gift in satisfaction of the confiscation order.

6.20   Once a confiscation order has been made and is not subject to appeal, the High Court and the county court have the power under the Drug Trafficking Act, on an application by the prosecutor, to appoint a receiver to realise (ie sell) any realisable property. Although both the High Court and the county court have this power, in practice it is preferable for the prosecutor to make application for the appointment of a receiver to the High Court.

6.21   Before any property is realised the court must give a reasonable opportunity to those holding any interest in the property, including the recipients of gifts caught by the Act, to make representations. The receiver will dispose of property, as necessary, and pay the monies raised to the enforcing Justices' Clerk in satisfaction of the confiscation order. Both the High Court and the county court can order persons who hold realisable property to give possession of it to the receiver, a power which may be employed to compel property to be brought into the jurisdiction.

6.22   Thus, some large confiscation orders may effectively be enforced by the prosecutor, the role of the Justices' Clerk being limited to receiving any monies raised by the receiver. Enquiries about this method of enforcement (which will normally involve only orders worth £10,000 or more) should be directed to:

Central Confiscation Branch,
Crown Prosecution Service,
50 Ludgate Hill,
London, EC4M 7EX (FAX 0171 273 1325);

or,depending on the case,

Asset Forfeiture Unit,
Solicitor's Office,
HM Customs and Excise,
New King's Beam House,
22 Upper Ground,
London, SE1 9PJ (FAX 0171 865 5902).

The principle in any case involving a receiver is that there should be close liaison at the enforcement stage between the prosecutor, the receiver and the enforcing magistrates' court. The enforcing magistrates' court should also contact the prosecutor in any case where there is a restraint or charging order in force.

Imprisonment in default

6.23   Because a confiscation order is treated in many ways as if it were a Crown Court fine, the Crown Court must, when making the order, specify a term of imprisonment in default of payment of the order. The relevant default terms are to be found in section 31(3A) of the Powers of Criminal Courts Act 1973. The maximum default term, in respect of unpaid sums over £1 million, is currently 10 years. A default term is to be served after any custodial sentence (other than a suspended sentence) imposed for the offence or offences of which the drug trafficker has been convicted, and is not to run concurrently.

6.24   The enforcing magistrates' court may commit a person to prison in default of payment, but before this is done all other methods of enforcing the order must have been attempted without success.

6.25   Furthermore, unlike fines, confiscation orders imposed under the Drug Trafficking Act or any amount still outstanding under them are not expunged by the service of a term of imprisonment in default. Such orders remain enforceable even after a default term has been served.

Inadequacy of realisable property

6.26   Where there is still a sum due for payment under a confiscation order and there is no further property available for enforcement, application should be made to the High Court by the defendant under section 17 of the Drug Trafficking Act, described in Chapter 8.19 below, for a certificate of inadequacy so that the Crown Court may reduce the amount to be recovered under the order to nil. Under the Drug Trafficking Act, it is also possible for a receiver appointed in the case to apply for a certificate of inadequacy.

6.27   The amount to be paid under a confiscation order may only be reduced by the Crown Court, on the basis of a certificate of inadequacy issued by the High Court under section 17 of the Drug Trafficking Act. Therefore, in order to show the enforcing magistrates' court that there is insufficient realisable property to satisfy the order and that a warrant of commitment should not be issued, it will be necessary for the defendant to show that a certificate has been obtained from the High Court under section 17.

6.28   The prosecutor will inform the Justices' Clerk of the enforcing magistrates' court of any application to the High Court for a certificate of inadequacy, and will discuss how enforcement should be handled pending the outcome of the application.

Enforcement against assets outside the jurisdiction

6.29   Both a restraint order and a confiscation order may take account of assets held by the defendant or a person to whom the defendant has made a gift caught by the Act which are located outside the jurisdiction. Where a restraint or confiscation order is made or is to be made affecting assets outside the jurisdiction, any necessary enforcement action will need to be taken in the country or territory in question, via the United Kingdom Central Authority in the Home Office. Chapters 21 and 22 contain further details.

6.30   Where a confiscation order is passed to another jurisdiction for enforcement, monies may not be forwarded to the enforcing Justices' Clerk in England and Wales because confiscated assets may be retained by the country where they are confiscated. By virtue of Articles 7 and 8 of the Drug Trafficking Offences Act 1986 (Designated Countries and Territories) Order 1990 (see Annex A), the amount payable under a confiscation order made in England and Wales is reduced by the value of any property confiscated abroad in satisfaction of the order.

6.31   A Justices' Clerk responsible for the enforcement of a confiscation order where there are assets abroad will therefore need to remain alert to the progress of proceedings in the country to which the confiscation order has been passed for enforcement.

7
Dead or absconded drug traffickers

7.1   Section 19 of the Drug Trafficking Act contains special provision for confiscating the proceeds of drug trafficking from dead or absconded drug traffickers. The legislation enables a confiscation order to be made in three situations:

  1.   where a person is convicted of a drug trafficking offence, and *dies* after conviction but before a confiscation order is made in the Crown Court;

  2.   where a person is convicted of a drug trafficking offence, and *absconds* after conviction but before a confiscation order is made in the Crown Court; and

  3.   where a person against whom proceedings have been instituted for a drug trafficking offence absconds *before* conviction.

Situation 1

7.2   Where a person dies after a confiscation order has been made against him or her, the order is enforceable against the estate of the deceased. The section 19 power caters for a different situation, where the defendant dies after conviction for a drug trafficking offence, but before a confiscation order can be made in the Crown Court.

7.3   Where this happens, section 19 enables the prosecutor to ask the High Court to exercise the powers of the Crown Court under the Drug Trafficking Act to make a confiscation order against the deceased defendant. The High Court has a discretion as to whether it exercises the powers.

Situation 2

7.3   Where a defendant absconds after conviction, but before a confiscation order can be made in the Crown Court, section 19 enables the prosecutor to apply to the High Court for a confiscation order to be made against the defendant. Again, the court has a discretion as to whether it makes an order or not.

7.4   It is important to note that the High Court may make a confiscation order against a convicted absconder **immediately** that person absconds, although the court must be satisfied that the prosecutor has taken reasonable steps to contact the absconder.

Situation 3

7.5   The prosecutor may also apply to the High Court to have a confiscation order made against a person **against whom proceedings have been instituted** who absconds **before** conviction. The High Court may not exercise these powers until the person in question has been an absconder for two years or more (compare this with the provisions on **convicted** absconders described above).

7.6   Furthermore, the Act makes it clear that the powers will only be exercisable where the relevant offences are committed on or after 3 February 1995, so there can be no confiscation orders against **unconvicted** absconders made before the spring of 1997. As with convicted absconders, the court must be satisfied that the prosecutor has taken reasonable steps to contact the absconder.

7.7 Arrangements have been made to notify persons charged with a drug trafficking offence on or after 3 February 1995 that a confiscation order may be made against them if they abscond. This is not a requirement of the Act but an additional measure to ensure that defendants are in no doubt as to the consequences of absconding.

Dead or absconded drug traffickers: general

7.8 The powers of the High Court under section 19 are the same as those available to the Crown Court, except that the High Court cannot make the required assumptions mentioned in section 4(2) of the Act and described in Chapter 5 above. The prosecutor is required to produce to the court a statement or statements under section 11 of the Act but the defendant, who will, of course, not be present at the proceedings, will not be required to respond to it. Any person appearing to the court to be likely to be affected by the making of a confiscation order is entitled to make representations before the court.

7.9 Orders made by the High Court under section 19 of the Act are enforced much as if they were drug trafficking confiscation orders made by the Crown Court following conviction. The exception to the normal practice is that only sections 31(1) and 32(1) of the Powers of Criminal Courts Act 1973 apply to orders made against dead drug traffickers. **In such cases, it is important that the High Court's attention is drawn to the need to specify an enforcing magistrates' court by order under section 31(1)(a) of the Powers of Criminal Courts Act 1973**.

7.10 The High Court should send full information about any confiscation order made both to the enforcing magistrates' court and, if the High Court's confiscation order follows proceedings against the defendant in the Crown Court, to the relevant Crown Court. Details of the information that should be provided are to be found in Chapter 6.8 and 6.9 above.

8
Revaluation

8.1   The Drug Trafficking Act 1994 envisages a number of circumstances under which a confiscation order may be made where none was made in the original proceedings, or a confiscation order that was made in the proceedings may be increased or decreased. The main thrust of the provisions is to enable proceeds and property which come to light only after the original confiscation order is made to be confiscated. The court procedures involved are triggered in most instances by the prosecutor.

(i)   Interest

Addition of interest to unpaid orders

8.2   As noted in Chapter 6, the Crown Court may allow the defendant time to pay the confiscation order. Payment may also be ordered forthwith, or by instalments. If the order is not paid in full by the time required, the defendant could draw interest on the unpaid amount.

8.3   In order to prevent the defendant from benefiting from failure to pay the confiscation order in full when required, section 10 of the Drug Trafficking Act provides that where a confiscation order is not paid by the allotted date the defendant must pay interest on the unpaid sum for the period for which it remains unpaid. Interest accrues automatically on all unpaid orders and the amount of the interest is to be treated for the purposes of enforcement as part of the amount to be recovered under the confiscation order. It will be appropriate for both the court imposing the order and the magistrates' court enforcing it to draw these provisions to the defendant's attention.

8.4   The interest accruing on unpaid confiscation orders is simple interest. Consequently, any payments received by a Justices' Clerk in satisfaction of an order will first act to reduce the principal sum owing. Interest will continue to accrue on the amount of the principal sum outstanding, but the interest already accrued will be treated as a separate amount on which no further interest can accrue. This points to the need, in practice, for Justices' Clerks to keep a separate note of the two amounts.

8.5   The rate of interest is that applicable for the time being to a civil judgment debt under section 17 of the Judgments Act 1838. The current rate is 8% per annum. Interest starts to accrue from the moment the order is not paid as required. In calculating the amount of interest the defendant is liable to pay, it will be appropriate to proceed on the basis of simple interest per annum, and the number of days for which payment of part or all of the confiscation order has been outstanding. The following formula will be appropriate:

Amount outstanding X number of days outstanding ÷ 365 X interest rate.

For example, A is given until 1 June to pay a confiscation order of £10,000 but defaults. The interest which has accrued is calculated 91 days later. The calculation will read:

$$10,000 \text{ X } 91 \div 365 \text{ X } 8 \div 100 = \text{£}199.$$

Total amount outstanding after 91 days: £10,199.

8.6　　The service of a term of imprisonment in default of a confiscation order does not affect the defendant's obligation to pay the order, and interest will continue to accrue on the unpaid element of a confiscation order during the service of a default term.

8.7　　Because interest increases the amount to be recovered under a confiscation order for enforcement purposes, the Crown Court may increase the term of imprisonment to be served by the defendant in default of payment of the confiscation order. Rule 33 of the Crown Court Rules 1982 as amended by the Crown Court (Amendment) Rules 1995 [SI 1995/2618(L.9)] lays down the procedure to be followed where the prosecutor applies to the Crown Court for an increase in the default term which the defendant will be required to serve.

(ii)　　*Realisable property*

Upward reassessment of realisable property

8.8　　Realisable property may only come to light after an offender has been tried and convicted and a confiscation order has been made. Consequently, the court may assess the offender's proceeds of drug trafficking correctly but decide that the amount that might be realised at the time is insufficient to satisfy a confiscation order in the full amount of the offender's proceeds. Under those circumstances, the amount to be recovered under the confiscation order will be set at a lower level than it might be.

8.9　　Alternatively, the amount that might be realised may be insufficient to satisfy a confiscation order in the full amount of the defendant's proceeds of drug trafficking at the time the order is made, but further realisable property may become available later which would permit property to the value of the full amount of the defendant's proceeds to be confiscated.

8.10　　Either of these situations could result in the value of the defendant's proceeds of crime not being confiscated. Section 16 of the Drug Trafficking Act, therefore, enables the High Court to issue a certificate giving the Crown Court the discretion to increase the amount to be recovered under a confiscation order made under the Drug Trafficking Act.

8.11　　The High Court will issue a certificate under section 16 where it is satisfied that the amount that might be realised at the time the confiscation order was made was greater than was thought at the time, or has subsequently increased.

8.12　　Application for a reconsideration of the amount that might be realised is made by the prosecutor or by a receiver appointed in the case, and must be made to the High Court. Application may be made at any time after the original confiscation order has been made.

8.13　　Where the High Court has issued a certificate, the prosecutor (but not a receiver) may then apply to the Crown Court for an increase in the amount to be recovered under the confiscation order. The Crown Court will decide what amount to substitute for the original one and will, if necessary, increase the default term to be served in the event of non-payment of the new amount of the confiscation order.

8.14　　The new amount to be recovered under the confiscation order under this procedure must not be greater than the amount of the defendant's proceeds of drug trafficking as originally assessed by the Crown Court. Section 16 is concerned with the amount of realisable property available, not with the value of the defendant's proceeds of drug trafficking. The question of the defendant's proceeds may be revisited using other procedures (see section (iii) of this chapter).

8.15   An example will illustrate the way section 16 works. At the time the confiscation order is made the Crown Court assesses the defendant's proceeds of drug trafficking at £100,000. It assesses the amount that might be realised, however, at only £50,000. The amount to be recovered from the defendant under the confiscation order is therefore set at £50,000.

8.16   The defendant then inherits £60,000. By virtue of section 16, this legacy may be taken into account and a certificate issued by the High Court stating that the amount that might be realised has increased to £110,000. The Crown Court may then increase the amount to be recovered under the confiscation order so that it is now £100,000.

8.17   Section 16 will not, however, apply so as to permit the increase of the amount to be recovered to £110,000 because that would exceed by £10,000 the level at which the Crown Court originally assessed the defendant's proceeds of drug trafficking.

8.18   The usual enforcement measures, including anticipatory restraint and charging orders, are available to ensure that the additional amount is realised.

Downward reassessment of realisable property

8.19   Section 17 of the Drug Trafficking Act enables the High Court to issue a certificate stating that there is insufficient realisable property available to satisfy any amount outstanding under a confiscation order. The person who applied for the certificate can then apply to the Crown Court which made the order to reduce the amount to be recovered under the order. The Crown Court exercises a discretion in deciding by how much the order should be reduced, taking account of all the circumstances.

8.20   Application for a certificate of inadequacy must be made to the High Court either by the defendant or by a receiver appointed in the case.

8.21   The term of imprisonment to be served in default of a confiscation order is linked to the size of the order. Therefore, where it reduces the amount to be recovered in accordance with a certificate issued by the High Court under section 17, the Crown Court must, if appropriate, substitute a lower term of imprisonment to be served in default of payment for the original one.

8.22   The burden of proof in an application under section 17 rests on the defendant (see Re F, the Times, 1 November 1994). An application will only succeed where it is clear that the proceeds of the realisation of all the defendant's property, together with the value of all gifts caught by the Act, are insufficient to allow the confiscation order to be paid in full.

8.23   This might happen, for example, where the Crown Court has overvalued an asset when assessing the amount that might be realised under the confiscation order. Or it might have considered that a gift made by the defendant to a third party was caught by the Act which the High Court, after hearing representations, decides was not.

Downward reassessment of realisable property: absconders

8.24   Section 21 of the Drug Trafficking Act makes special provision for absconders to apply to the High Court for a downward reassessment of the amount to be recovered under the confiscation order. The section has effect only where the High Court has made a confiscation order against a person who absconds before conviction and subsequently returns. Consequently, the powers will not come into play before 1997.

(iii)   Proceeds

Upward reassessment of proceeds: general

8.25   The proceeds of drug trafficking may only come to light after the trial. Consequently, the prosecutor and the Crown Court may decide not to trigger the confiscation procedures following the defendant's conviction. Or then again, the confiscation procedures may be triggered but the court may conclude that the defendant did not benefit from drug trafficking. Or the court may decide that the defendant's proceeds of drug trafficking were lower than they really were.

8.26   Provision to deal with all three situations is contained in sections 13 to 15 of the Drug Trafficking Act. Here it is not the amount of realisable property that the court has an opportunity to re-examine but the question of whether the defendant benefited from drug trafficking and the extent of the defendant's proceeds of drug trafficking.

8.27   Under sections 13 to 15, application is made to the Crown Court by the prosecutor and an application may be entertained by the court if it is made within 6 years of the defendant's conviction. The prosecutor must provide the court with a section 11 statement in all cases and the court can also require the defendant to provide information under section 12 of the Act. The usual enforcement powers, including pre-emptive restraint and charging orders to prevent the dissipation of assets, are available to support the prosecutor's application for revaluation.

8.28   No payment or reward received by the defendant on or after the date of conviction may be taken into account unless the prosecutor can show that it was received by the defendant in connection with drug trafficking carried on by the defendant or another person *on or before the date of conviction.* When dealing with an application under sections 13 to 15 of the Drug Trafficking Act, the court is not allowed to make the assumptions described in section 4 of the Act in respect of payments or rewards received by the defendant *on or after the date of conviction.*

Situation 1: confiscation procedures were not triggered

8.29   Section 13 covers the situation where the confiscation procedures were not triggered when the defendant originally appeared in the Crown Court for sentence and so the court did not get as far as determining whether the defendant had benefited from drug trafficking. If the prosecutor has evidence **which was not available to him/her when the defendant was sentenced** which he/she believes would have led the court to believe that the defendant had benefited from drug trafficking, the prosecutor may ask the Crown Court to consider the evidence.

8.30   After the prosecutor has made an application, a good deal of discretion is left to the court. The court will only proceed if it is satisfied that it is appropriate to do so. In so deciding, it must have regard to all the circumstances of the case. If it decides to make a confiscation order, it must order the payment of whatever sum it thinks just in all the circumstances of the case, and in considering the circumstances it is required to have regard to any fine previously imposed on the defendant in respect of the offence or offences in question.

Situation 2: court thought the defendant had not benefited

8.31   Section 14 covers the situation where the confiscation procedures were triggered either in the Crown Court or the High Court but the court determined that the defendant had not benefited from drug trafficking (and so no confiscation order was made). If the prosecutor has evidence **not previously considered by the court** but which the prosecutor believes would have led the court to determine that the defendant did in fact benefit from drug trafficking, he/she may ask the Crown Court to consider it.

8.32   If the Crown Court is satisfied that it would have determined that the defendant did benefit from drug trafficking if the new evidence had been available to it, it will make a fresh determination of the defendant's proceeds of drug trafficking and may impose a confiscation order.

8.33   Section 14 does not apply where the High Court was asked to consider making a confiscation order against an absconder but decided not to do so, for as long as the person in question remains an absconder. It does, however, apply where the High Court has determined that an absconder did not benefit from drug trafficking, and the absconder returns.

Situation 3: court made a confiscation order

8.34   Thirdly, there is the situation where the Crown Court or the High Court determined that a person had benefited from drug trafficking, assessed the proceeds and the amount that might be realised and made a confiscation order (including a confiscation order in a nominal amount, where such an order is made). Where the prosecutor is of the opinion that the real value of the defendant's proceeds of drug trafficking was greater than their assessed value, he/she may apply to the Crown Court for the evidence on which that opinion has been formed to be considered by the court. More than one revaluation may be made under section 15.

8.35   Having considered the evidence, the Crown Court will then make a fresh determination if it is satisfied that the real value of the defendant's proceeds of drug trafficking was greater than was thought when the previous determination was made. This may be either because the real value of the proceeds was greater than was thought at the time or because the value of the proceeds in question has subsequently increased. For example, the defendant may have received gold in return for drugs. At the time the confiscation order was made the gold may have been worth less than it is now.

8.36   Having made the fresh determination, the Crown Court will check whether the new amount at which it has reassessed the defendant's proceeds of drug trafficking exceeds the court's original assessment. If it does, it may substitute for the original amount to be recovered under the confiscation order whatever new amount it thinks just in all the circumstances of the case. Where the court increases the amount to be recovered it will need, where appropriate, to increase the term of imprisonment to be served in default.

8.37   Section 15 of the Act does not apply where the High Court has made a confiscation order against an absconder, as long as the person in question remains an absconder. It does, however, apply where the High Court has made a confiscation order against an absconder, and the absconder returns.

Downward reassessment of proceeds

8.38   Section 21 of the Drug Trafficking Act permits the defendant's proceeds of drug trafficking to be reassessed downwards. It applies where the defendant absconds before conviction, a confiscation order is made by the High Court, and the defendant then returns.

8.39   Application must be made to the High Court within 6 years of the date on which the confiscation order was made. If the High Court accepts the defendant's allegation that his/her proceeds of drug trafficking were less than the High Court believed when it made the confiscation order, the court will make a fresh determination. If it varies the amount to be recovered, it must, if appropriate, substitute a lower term of imprisonment to be served in default for the original one.

Conclusion

8.40   The discovery of further assets after a drug trafficking conviction may lead both to a reassessment of the defendant's proceeds of drug trafficking and to a reassessment of the amount of realisable property available for enforcement. The prosecutor will need to consider very carefully which application is appropriate in the circumstances of a particular case.

SECTION 3
ALL CRIME CONFISCATION IN ENGLAND AND WALES

9

Investigations into the proceeds of crime

9.1   The Drug Trafficking Act 1994 contains particular powers, described in Chapter 3, for use in investigations into drug trafficking. There are also special powers, described in Chapter 15, to assist in investigations into terrorist finances.

9.2   Until 1995, however, financial investigators interested in the proceeds of other crimes had to rely on the powers to gain access to special procedure material afforded by Schedule 1 to the Police and Criminal Evidence Act 1984 ("PACE"). Schedule 1 of PACE empowers Circuit judges to make production orders and issue search warrants in respect of confidential banking and other material, but the powers are not as useful in asset tracing investigations as sections 55 and 56 of the Drug Trafficking Act because, for instance:

- there must be reasonable grounds for believing that a "serious arrestable offence", as defined by PACE, has been committed;

- the application for a production order is *inter partes,* that is to say the person or body to produce the material may be present at and contest the application;

- the material to be produced must be relevant evidence.

9.3   Part VI of the Criminal Justice Act 1988 contains England and Wales's all crime confiscation legislation. Sections 93H and 93I of the 1988 Act, added by the Proceeds of Crime Act 1995, create, respectively, new powers to make a production order and issue a search warrant for the purpose of an investigation into criminal conduct generally similar to those at sections 55 and 56 of the Drug Trafficking Act with respect to drug trafficking. The new powers became available on 1 November 1995.

9.4   The new all crime investigative powers are, however, more tightly circumscribed than those in the drug trafficking legislation. Whereas the drug trafficking investigative powers are available for use in investigations into "drug trafficking" (ie all aspects of drug trafficking), the new all crime investigative powers are restricted to "an investigation into whether any person has benefited from any criminal conduct or into the extent or whereabouts of the proceeds of any criminal conduct".

9.5   "Criminal conduct" is defined by section 93A(7) of the Criminal Justice Act 1988 (as added by the Criminal Justice Act 1993) as conduct which constitutes an offence to which Part VI of the Criminal Justice Act 1988 applies or would constitute such an offence if it had occurred in England and Wales or (as the case may be) Scotland. Part VI of the Criminal Justice Act 1988 applies to offences listed in Schedule 4 to that Act and to all indictable offences except drug trafficking offences and offences under Part III of the Prevention of Terrorism (Temporary Provisions) Act 1989, which are covered by other legislation.

9.6   By virtue of the definition of "criminal conduct", the all crime investigative powers in sections 93H and 93I of the Criminal Justice Act 1988 are available for use in this country to assist overseas investigations in relation to acquisitive crime generally, just as those at sections 55 and 56 of the Drug Trafficking Act may be used to assist overseas drug trafficking investigations.

Financial Investigators

9.7   As noted in Chapter 3.25, the National Criminal Intelligence Service holds details of United Kingdom Financial Investigators (primarily Financial Investigators working in the Metropolitan Police, other police forces, Regional Crime Squads and HM Customs and Excise). It also holds details of Money Laundering Reporting Officers working in financial institutions (see Chapter 17.6 below). These schedules are regularly updated and forwarded annually to all banks and forces.

10
The preservation of assets

Restraint and charging orders

10.1   Both the restraint order and charging order are available to prevent the dissipation of property so that it is available to satisfy an all crime confiscation order that has been or may be made. The form and function of restraint and charging orders under Part VI of the Criminal Justice Act 1988 are the same as restraint and charging orders under the Drug Trafficking Act, described in Chapter 4.

10.2   Like restraint and charging orders under the drug trafficking legislation, restraint and charging orders under Part VI of the Criminal Justice Act 1988 may be made where proceedings are instituted, or just before, and have not been concluded. The powers are also available to support applications for revaluation, as described in Chapter 14.

Disclosure of information held by Government departments

10.3   Section 13 of the Proceeds of Crime Act 1995 adds a new section 93J to the Criminal Justice Act 1988 to enable material held by a government department to be produced to the High Court, and to be disclosed on the court's order. The provisions are closely modelled on those in section 59 of the Drug Trafficking Act 1994, described in detail in Chapter 4 above, and have been available for use since 1 November 1995.

Delay in notifying arrest

10.4   Section 99 of the Criminal Justice Act 1988 amends the Police and Criminal Evidence Act 1984 so that delay in notifying arrest, or delay in access to legal advice on arrest, may be authorised where proceeds might otherwise be dissipated.

10.5   The conditions are that the offence is one to which Part VI of the 1988 Act applies, and that an officer has reasonable grounds to believe that the detained person has benefited from the offence and that the recovery of the value of the property obtained from the offence, or the pecuniary advantage obtained from it, will be hindered by disclosing the fact of the arrest. As with the drug trafficking provisions, these powers enable a restraint or charging order to be obtained urgently before the defendant has the opportunity to dissipate assets, or instruct associates to do so.

Bankruptcy, insolvency and liquidation

10.6   The Criminal Justice Act 1988 also contains provision similar to that described in Chapter 4 to cover the situation where the same person is the subject of both confiscation and insolvency proceedings.

11
The crime confiscation order

11.1   Part VI of the Criminal Justice Act 1988 enables the courts to confiscate the proceeds of all offences listed in Schedule 4 to the Act and of all indictable offences other than drug trafficking offences and offences under Part III of the Prevention of Terrorism (Temporary Provisions) Act 1989. **Like a confiscation order under the Drug Trafficking Act, a confiscation order under Part VI of the Criminal Justice Act 1988 is an order to pay a sum of money, expressed in sterling. It is not an order transferring the title of property**.

11.2   The Proceeds of Crime Act 1995 brings Part VI of the Criminal Justice Act 1988 more closely into line with the drug trafficking confiscation legislation. There are, however, still a number of important differences between the two schemes. One is that a drug trafficking confiscation order can be made by the Crown Court or the High Court. A confiscation order under Part VI of the Criminal Justice Act 1988 can be made by the Crown Court or a magistrates' court.

11.3   The magistrates' court has the power to make a confiscation order under the 1988 Act where the defendant is convicted in the magistrates' court of one or more of the offences listed in Schedule 4 to the Act. The magistrates' court has no power to make a confiscation order where the defendant is convicted in the magistrates' court of an either way or summary offence which is not listed in Schedule 4 to the 1988 Act.

11.4   The list of offences in Schedule 4 to the 1988 Act was extended by the Criminal Justice Act 1988 (Confiscation Orders) Order 1990 [SI 1990/1570], the Criminal Justice Act 1988 (Confiscation Orders) Order 1995 [S.I. 1995/3145] and the Criminal Justice Act 1988 (Confiscation Orders) Order 1996 [S.I. 1996/1716]. Practitioners should be alert to the possibility of further amending Orders.

11.5   The Crown Court has the power to make a confiscation order under Part VI of the Criminal Justice Act 1988 where the defendant is found guilty in the Crown Court of any offence to which Part VI of the Criminal Justice Act 1988 applies.

Which version of the 1988 Act applies?

11.6   Part VI of the Criminal Justice Act 1988 came into force on 3 April 1989. It was amended by sections 27 and 28 of the Criminal Justice Act 1993. Part VI of the 1988 Act as amended by those sections applies to any case where the proceedings were instituted on or after 3 February 1995.

11.7   Part VI of the 1988 Act was further amended, as of 1 November 1995, by the Proceeds of Crime Act 1995. The 1988 Act as further amended by the 1995 Act took effect on 1 November 1995, and the new confiscation procedures introduced by the Proceeds of Crime Act apply only where all the offences of which the defendant is convicted were committed on or after 1 November 1995.

11.8   As with the drug trafficking confiscation law, this section of the guide describes the latest version of the legislation. It explains the operation of Part VI of the Criminal Justice Act 1988 as amended both by the Criminal Justice Act 1993 and the

Proceeds of Crime Act 1995. This chapter does not apply to Part VI of the Criminal Justice Act 1988 prior to the amendments made to it by the Criminal Justice Act 1993 and the Proceeds of Crime Act 1995. The 1988 Act confiscation procedures, as amended by the 1993 Act but not the 1995 Act, remain in force for use in cases where all or some of the offences of which the defendant is convicted were committed before 1 November 1995.

Sequence of the 1988 Act procedures

11.9   Like a drug trafficking confiscation order, a confiscation order under Part VI of the Criminal Justice Act 1988 can only be made after a relevant conviction. As with the drug trafficking legislation, the confiscation procedures are triggered by the prosecutor, or by the court of its own volition. The procedure under the 1988 Act is slightly different in that the prosecutor is required to trigger the procedures by submitting written notice. An oral request is not sufficient.

Factors relevant to whether the procedures should be triggered

11.10   The statutory minimum amount of a confiscation order under the 1988 Act (£10,000) was abolished by the Proceeds of Crime Act 1995. However, it will not normally be appropriate for the confiscation procedures to be triggered unless there is a realistic prospect of a confiscation order of £10,000 or more being made. Where it seems likely that the final amount of the order will fall below this sum, the following factors will be particularly relevant in considering whether confiscation proceedings should be mounted:

- whether the facts of the case make confiscation particularly appropriate, even though the order might be for less than £10,000;

- how far under £10,000 the order would be;

- whether it will be feasible to enforce the order if made;

- how easily realisable the assets are;

- whether an assessment of the likely overall costs (including court time, legal aid and prosecution costs) indicates that they are proportionate to the amount that will be realised.

Postponement

11.11   Section 72A of the 1988 Act (as inserted by section 28 of the Criminal Justice Act 1993) permits both the Crown Court and a magistrates' court to postpone confiscation whilst proceeding to sentence the defendant.

11.12   The postponement provisions are very similar to those in the Drug Trafficking Act which are described in Chapter 5 above. The time limits which apply to postponements under the Criminal Justice Act 1988 are the same as under the Drug Trafficking Act. These are that the court's consideration of the confiscation matters will not normally be postponed for more than 6 months after the date of conviction. Where the defendant has appealed against conviction the postponement will not normally be longer than 3 months after the date on which the appeal is determined or otherwise disposed of.

11.13   The procedures to be followed in connection with postponement in the Crown Court under the Criminal Justice Act 1988 are contained in the Crown Court Rules 1982 as amended by the Crown Court (Amendment) (No.2) Rules 1994 [S.I. 1994/3153 (L.19)]. For the magistrates' court see the Magistrates' Courts (Miscellaneous Amendments) Rules 1994 [S.I. 1994/3154 (L.20)].

The determination of benefit

11.14   Once the prosecutor has triggered the confiscation procedures or the court has decided to proceed of its own volition, the issues before it are much the same as under the Drug Trafficking Act, as described in Chapter 5 above.

11.15   There is, however, one fundamental difference between the two schemes: in assessing the defendant's proceeds of drug trafficking under the drug trafficking legislation, the assumptions (see Chapter 5) must be made in every case. Under Part VI of the Criminal Justice Act 1988, the assumptions may only be made where the prosecutor's notice triggering the confiscation procedures contains a declaration that the case is appropriate for them, and there are other preconditions, described below. The court has no power under the 1988 Act to make the assumptions of its own volition.

11.16   Once the confiscation procedures have been triggered under the 1988 Act, the court must first consider whether the defendant has benefited from any "relevant criminal conduct". In a confiscation case in the magistrates' court, "relevant criminal conduct" means any offences listed in Schedule 4 to the 1988 Act of which the defendant has been convicted in the current proceedings, plus any other such offences taken into consideration by the court in those proceedings. In a confiscation case in the Crown Court, "relevant criminal conduct" means any offences to which Part VI of the 1988 Act applies, plus any other such offences taken into consideration by the court in those proceedings.

11.17   **By virtue of section 72AA(6) of the 1988 Act, "relevant criminal conduct" also includes offences of which the defendant need not have been convicted, but from which the defendant is assumed to have benefited, in cases where the assumptions are made.**

11.18   Section 71(7A) of the Criminal Justice Act 1988 makes it clear that the standard of proof applicable in determining any question of benefit or of the amount to be recovered is the civil standard (the balance of probabilities).

11.19   In cases in the Crown Court not involving the assumptions, the defendant's benefit from relevant criminal conduct will be the total benefit from all the offences of which the defendant has been convicted and to which Part VI of the 1988 Act applies, plus the benefit from any other such offences which the court takes into consideration. In cases in the magistrates' court not involving the assumptions, the defendant's benefit from relevant criminal conduct will be the total benefit from all the Schedule 4 offences of which the defendant has been convicted, plus the benefit from any other such offences which the court takes into consideration.

The assumptions

11.20   As mentioned in paragraph 11.17, by virtue of section 72AA(6) of the 1988 Act, "relevant criminal conduct" includes offences from which the defendant is assumed to have benefited, in cases where the court makes the assumptions set out in section 72AA of the 1988 Act. Much as in the Drug Trafficking Act, the assumptions are primarily that all property held by the defendant on conviction, plus all property which passed through the defendant's hands in the six years before the institution of proceedings, came from relevant criminal conduct.

11.21   If the defendant is unable to rebut the assumptions, the court can assess the defendant's benefit from relevant criminal conduct at the total amount of assumed benefit revealed by the assumptions and, subject to the realisable property available for confiscation, order the defendant to pay that amount.

11.22   Under the Drug Trafficking Act, the court must make the assumptions in every case, even where the defendant appears for sentence in respect of a single first time drug trafficking offence. The court may only make the assumptions under the 1988 Act where the defendant is convicted of two or more relevant offences in the current proceedings, or one relevant offence in the current proceedings and has a previous conviction of another relevant offence in the last six years. This is one of a number of features built into the 1988 Act to ensure that the assumptions are not made in trivial cases.

11.23   The detailed requirements are as follows. The *Crown Court* can make the assumptions where either of the following sets of conditions is satisfied: *either* the defendant must have been convicted in the current proceedings of two or more offences to which Part VI of the Criminal Justice Act 1988 applies, both committed on or after 1 November 1995 and from which the defendant has benefited; *or* the defendant must have been convicted of at least one such offence in the current proceedings, and have another conviction of such an offence in previous proceedings in the last six years (whether before the Crown Court or a magistrates' court). In the case of the second set of conditions, the previous offence must also have been committed on or after 1 November 1995.

11.24   The *magistrates' court* can make the assumptions where either of the following sets of conditions is satisfied: *either* the defendant must have been convicted in the current proceedings of one offence listed in Schedule 4 to the Criminal Justice Act 1988 plus one other offence to which Part VI of the Criminal Justice Act 1988 applies, both committed on or after 1 November 1995 and from which the defendant has benefited; *or* the defendant must have been convicted in the current proceedings of one Schedule 4 offence committed on or after 1 November 1995 and from which the defendant has benefited, and have another conviction in the last six years of any offence to which Part VI of the Criminal Justice Act 1988 applies (whether before the Crown Court or a magistrates' court), again committed on or after 1 November 1995 and from which the defendant has benefited.

11.25   It will be noted that there must always be a conviction of at least one Schedule 4 offence in the current proceedings before the magistrates' court can make the assumptions. Once the preconditions are satisfied, however, the magistrates' court makes exactly the same assumptions as the Crown Court.

11.26   An important feature of the 1988 Act is that the court is under no obligation to make the assumptions if it does not think fit to do so. However, once the court has decided to make the assumptions in a case to which the 1988 Act applies, it will make all the assumptions set out in section 72AA(4) of the Act.

Statements relating to crime

11.27   Like the Drug Trafficking Act, Part VI of the Criminal Justice Act 1988 provides for the prosecutor to supply the court with information about the defendant's benefit from relevant criminal conduct in the form of a prosecutor's statement under section 73 of the Act.

11.28   The prosecutor must supply the court with a statement in all cases, where triggering the confiscation procedures, and may be required to produce one or more further statements. The court may also require the prosecutor to produce a statement or statements where it proceeds of its own volition.

11.29   The defendant may tender to the court a statement about his/her realisable property and the court may treat any acceptance by the prosecutor of an allegation in such a statement as conclusive of the matters to which it relates.

11.30   Rules of Court cover the procedure to be followed in respect of statements under section 73 of the 1988 Act as they affect both the Crown Court and magistrates' courts. They are the Crown Court (Amendment) Rules 1995 [SI 1995/2618(L.9)] and the Magistrates' Courts (Amendment) (No.2) Rules 1995 [SI 1995/2619(L.10)].

Order to defendant to provide information

11.31   Section 73A of the Criminal Justice Act 1988 enables the court, where the confiscation procedures have been triggered, to order the defendant to give it any information it thinks fit to assist it in carrying out its functions under Part VI of the Criminal Justice Act 1988. If the defendant fails to produce the information required within the time specified by the court, it may draw such inferences as it thinks fit.

The amount that might be realised

11.32   Once the court has determined that the defendant has benefited from relevant criminal conduct and the value of that benefit, it must then determine the amount to be recovered under the confiscation order and order the defendant to pay that amount. The value of the order will be equal to the amount of the defendant's benefit or to the amount which might be realised, whichever is less.

11.33   In other words, where the amount that might be realised is equal to, or more than the value of the defendant's benefit from relevant criminal conduct, the amount of the confiscation order will be that of the defendant's benefit. Where the amount that might be realised is less than the defendant's benefit, the court will order the defendant to pay a sum equal to the amount that might be realised.

11.34   As in the Drug Trafficking Act, "the amount that might be realised" is defined as realisable property held by the defendant, minus obligations having priority, plus gifts caught by the 1988 Act.

11.35   The definition of a gift caught by the 1988 Act is not quite the same as a gift caught by the Drug Trafficking Act. A gift is caught by the 1988 Act when it is made after the commission of the earliest offence to which the proceedings relate, or the date of the earliest offence taken into consideration in determining a convicted person's sentence. Furthermore, a gift is caught by the 1988 Act only if the court considers it appropriate in all the circumstances to take it into account.

12

The confiscation/compensation relationship

12.1   Where many crimes are concerned, there will be a clearly identifiable victim. If the defendant's assets were paid to the Crown in satisfaction of a confiscation order the victim could be disadvantaged. Part VI of the Criminal Justice Act 1988 therefore contains provision to ensure that the position of victims is safeguarded.

12.2   Firstly, many criminal offences are also torts. The victim of an offence may mount an action against the offender in the civil courts. Consequently, section 71(1C) of the 1988 Act replaces the court's obligation to make a confiscation order with a discretionary power to do so where the court is satisfied that the victim of any relevant criminal conduct has instituted, or intends to institute, civil proceedings against the defendant in respect of loss, injury or damage sustained in connection with that conduct.

12.3   Furthermore, a criminal court may order the offender to pay compensation to a victim under the Powers of Criminal Courts Act 1973. Compensation orders under the 1973 Act may in themselves provide an effective means of depriving an offender of the proceeds of an offence. Many of the offences to which Part VI of the Criminal Justice Act 1988 applies will naturally attract the imposition of a compensation order making redress to the victim. Therefore, the 1988 Act also contains provision covering the relationship between confiscation orders and compensation orders under the Powers of Criminal Courts Act.

12.4   The court may make both a confiscation order under Part VI of the Criminal Justice Act 1988 and a compensation order under the Powers of Criminal Courts Act 1973 against the same defendant in the same proceedings. Where it appears that the defendant has insufficient means to pay both orders, section 72(7) of the 1988 Act applies. Under this section, the court may order any shortfall in payment of the compensation order to be paid out of the monies raised by the enforcement of the confiscation order. An example will illustrate how the section works.

12.5   It may be assumed for this purpose that the defendant has benefited from certain offences to the tune of £12,000 and the amount that might be realised is £15,000. The court makes a confiscation order for £12,000. In addition, the court orders the offender to pay £5,000 to a victim. The total value of the two orders is £17,000 but there is only £15,000 worth of realisable property available to satisfy them.

12.6   If the confiscation order is satisfied in full only £3,000 remains for the compensation order, but the court has ordered the payment of £5,000 compensation. By virtue of section 72(7) the court is able to direct that the shortfall of £2,000 is to be paid out of the sums realised under the confiscation order. In effect the confiscation order is satisfied only to the extent of £10,000, the remaining £2,000 going to the victim.

12.7   These provisions are important because they bring the additional powers available for enforcing confiscation orders to bear on behalf of the victim. Thus, the recipient of the compensation order is not disadvantaged by the making of the confiscation order. Indeed, the victim will have the benefit of a share in assets identified and recovered under the confiscation procedures.

13

The enforcement of all crime confiscation orders

13.1   Justices' Clerks are responsible for enforcing confiscation orders made under Part VI of the Criminal Justice Act 1988. As with drug trafficking confiscation orders, the enforcement of which is described in Chapter 6, once they have made any deductions authorised by the statute, they pay the residue of monies received in satisfaction of a confiscation order to the Lord Chancellor for onward transmission to the Consolidated Fund.

13.2   Like drug trafficking confiscation orders, confiscation orders made by the Crown Court under Part VI of the Criminal Justice Act 1988 are enforced in many ways like Crown Court fines. Therefore, sections 31(1) to (3C) and 32(1) and (2) of the Powers of Criminal Courts Act 1973 and Part III of the Magistrates' Courts Act 1980 have effect, as described in Chapter 6.

13.3   A confiscation order made by a magistrates' court under Part VI of the 1988 Act is treated for enforcement purposes as if it were a fine imposed by the magistrates' court. By virtue of section 75(2) of the 1988 Act, however, section 31(3) of the Magistrates' Courts Act 1980 has effect in relation to confiscation orders made in the magistrates' court. Consequently, the normal limits on the magistrates' powers to imprison do not apply to imprisonment in default of a confiscation order.

13.4   An additional method of enforcement, as in the Drug Trafficking Act, is by the appointment of a receiver on the application of the prosecutor. The same criteria apply as set out in Chapter 6. In addition to the contact points mentioned in Chapter 6.22, enforcement authorities may wish to note the following contact point for enquiries in receivership cases dealt with by the Department of Social Security:

> **Office of the Solicitor,**
> **Department of Social Security,**
> **New Court,**
> **48 Carey Street,**
> **London, WC2A 2LS (FAX 0171 412 1317).**

13.5   Like a confiscation order under the Drug Trafficking Act, a confiscation order under Part VI of the Criminal Justice Act 1988 is not expunged by the service of a term of imprisonment in default, and remains enforceable by other means.

Payment of compensation out of confiscation order

13.6   As explained in Chapter 12, the Criminal Justice Act 1988 provides, under certain circumstances, for the Justices' Clerk enforcing the confiscation order to pay sums owing under a compensation order out of monies realised in satisfaction of a confiscation order made in the same proceedings.

13.7   Under section 81 of the 1988 Act, the Justices' Clerk is empowered to deduct the cost of realisation from the amount of compensation paid so the amount the victim receives is net of realisation costs. The principle is the same as that governing confiscation orders. Just as the receiver's expenses are met out of the gross monies paid to the Justices' Clerk by a receiver, so are the costs of realising the sum paid out in compensation.

Enforcement against assets outside the jurisdiction

13.8   Both a restraint order and a confiscation order under Part VI of the Criminal Justice Act 1988 may take account of assets held by the defendant or a person to whom the defendant has made a gift caught by the Act which are located outside the jurisdiction. Where a restraint or confiscation order is made or to be made affecting assets outside the jurisdiction, any necessary enforcement action will need to be taken in the country or territory in question, via the United Kingdom Central Authority in the Home Office. Chapters 21 and 22 contain further details.

13.9   Where a confiscation order is passed to another jurisdiction for enforcement, any confiscated assets may be retained by the country where they are confiscated. By virtue of Articles 7 and 8 of the Criminal Justice Act 1988 (Designated Countries and Territories) Order 1991 [S.I. 1991/2873] (see Annex A), the amount payable under a confiscation order made in England and Wales is reduced by the value of any property confiscated abroad in satisfaction of the order.

13.10   A Justices' Clerk responsible for the enforcement of a confiscation order where there are assets abroad will therefore need to remain alert to the progress of proceedings in the country to which the confiscation order has been passed for enforcement.

14
Revaluation

14.1   Revaluation provisions similar to those in the Drug Trafficking Act are available for use in relation to confiscation orders made under Part VI of the Criminal Justice Act 1988.

(i)   Interest

Addition of interest to unpaid orders

14.2   Section 75A of the Criminal Justice Act 1988 provides that interest shall be added to confiscation orders under the 1988 Act which are not paid as required by the court. The position is similar to that described in Chapter 8 in relation to the addition of interest to drug trafficking confiscation orders.

14.3   Where interest is added to a confiscation order made by the Crown Court under Part VI of the Criminal Justice Act 1988, the term of imprisonment in default may be increased accordingly. Procedures governing the prosecutor's application for an increase in the default term are set out in the Crown Court (Amendment) Rules 1995 [S.I. 1995/2618(L.9)].

(ii)   Realisable property

Downward reassessment of realisable property

14.4   Under section 83 of the 1988 Act the defendant or a receiver may apply to the High Court for a certificate indicating that the realisable property is inadequate to satisfy any amount remaining to be recovered under the confiscation order. The criteria to be applied by the High Court in addressing an application under section 83 of the 1988 Act are the same as those applicable under section 17 of the Drug Trafficking Act 1994, described in Chapter 8.

14.5   If the High Court is prepared to issue a certificate, the Crown Court may, on application by the defendant or receiver, reduce the amount to be recovered under the confiscation order. It will, if appropriate, also substitute a lower default term for the original one. If the confiscation order was made by a magistrates' court, a magistrates' court for the same area may reduce the amount to be recovered under the order.

(iii) Proceeds

Upward reassessment of proceeds

14.6   Sections 74A, 74B and 74C of the Criminal Justice Act 1988 enable the court to consider or revisit, on the application of the prosecutor, the question of the defendant's benefit from any relevant criminal conduct at any time within six years after conviction. Like the other confiscation provisions in Part VI of the Criminal Justice Act 1988 as amended by the Proceeds of Crime Act, the powers apply only where the offences in respect of which the defendant was originally found guilty were committed on or after 1 November 1995.

14.7   The purpose of the provisions is to enable the court to make a confiscation order where none was made in the original proceedings, or to increase an order already made. The powers are available to both the Crown Court and the magistrates' court. One context in which they will be relevant is where criminals benefit from their crimes by the issue of books, films and similar material in the media.

14.8   Section 74A applies where the confiscation procedures were not triggered in the original proceedings because the prosecutor did not give the court notice, or the court did not decide to proceed of its own volition. Section 74B applies where the court did proceed in the original proceedings, but determined that the defendant had not benefited from any relevant criminal conduct. In both cases, the court, by applying the revaluation powers, can make a confiscation order where none was made in the original proceedings.

14.9   Section 74C applies where a confiscation order has already been made, whether in the original proceedings or under new section 73A or 73B of the 1988 Act. It enables the court to increase the confiscation order already made by reference to the further proceeds uncovered. A confiscation order may be increased more than once under section 74C.

14.10   Much the same conditions apply to each of new sections 74A, 74B and 74C. The prosecutor must apply to the Crown Court or, where the proceedings were in the magistrates' court, to any magistrates' court for the same area. The evidence which the prosecutor applies to the court to consider must be new, and the court has a discretion to order the payment of such sum as it thinks just (not exceeding the defendant's benefit from relevant criminal conduct).

SECTION 4
TERRORIST FUNDS

15
Terrorist funds

15.1   The scheme for the forfeiture of funds associated with terrorism, which operates throughout the United Kingdom, is contained in the Prevention of Terrorism (Temporary Provisions) Act 1989. Until August 1996 there was also a separate scheme for the confiscation of such funds, which applied only to Northern Ireland. These provisions were found in the Northern Ireland (Emergency Provisions) Act 1991. However, they have now been repealed and superseded by the Proceeds of Crime (Northern Ireland) Order 1996. Further details of the Order are given in Chapter 20.

(i)   *Forfeiture*

15.2   Part III of the Prevention of Terrorism (Temporary Provisions) Act 1989 creates a number of criminal offences associated with the financing of terrorist groups or their activities. It also enables the courts to order the forfeiture of money or property used in these offences. The Act provides, in Schedule 4, a scheme for the enforcement of forfeiture orders, including a power to restrain property liable to forfeiture. It also provides enhanced investigative powers, in Part V and Schedule 7, which may be used for investigations into terrorist finances.

The forfeiture power

15.3   The forfeiture power in section 13 of the Prevention of Terrorism Act is triggered when a person is convicted of one of the Part III offences:

> **section 9   contributions towards acts of terrorism:** This section makes it an offence to solicit, receive, give or make available money or other property intending, knowing or having reasonable cause to suspect that it will be used in furtherance of acts of Northern Irish or international terrorism. The Criminal Justice Act 1993 extends section 9 to cover the possession or use of money or property in such circumstances;

> **section 10   contributions to proscribed organisations:** This section makes it an offence to solicit, receive, give or make available money or other property knowing or having reasonable cause to suspect that it is for the benefit of a proscribed terrorist organisation. The Criminal Justice Act 1993 extends the offence to cover the possession or use of such money or property;

> **section 11   assisting in the retention or control of terrorist funds:** This makes it an offence to assist another person to retain or control terrorist funds, which may be funds to be used in furtherance of terrorism, the proceeds of acts of terrorism, or the resources of proscribed terrorist organisations.

15.4   Under section 13 of the Act, the court may, in addition to imposing a prison sentence or fine on a person convicted of one of these offences, order the forfeiture of money or property associated with the offence. Forfeiture may only be applied in respect of money or property which the court considers may be used for terrorist purposes. The court is allowed to assume that it will be so used, unless evidence is produced to the contrary.

15.5   Forfeiture orders are enforced in accordance with Schedule 4, which sets out separate schemes in relation to England and Wales, Scotland and Northern Ireland. Schedule 4 allows the court, in making a forfeiture order, to make a further order directing that money or property is handed over to the court or the police; that it is paid to another person the court considers to be the owner of, or have an interest in, it; or that property is disposed of in a certain manner and the proceeds of disposal paid to the court. Where the property consists of land, the court may order the appointment of a receiver (or, in Scotland, an administrator) to take care of its disposal.

Restraint Orders

15.6   Schedule 4 also creates a power for the High Court (or, in Scotland, the Court of Session) to order the restraint of property which is or may be the subject of a forfeiture order under section 13. Schedule 4 contains provisions which ensure that a forfeiture order made in one jurisdiction of the United Kingdom is enforceable throughout the United Kingdom.

Investigative powers

15.7   Section 17 and Schedule 7 of the Prevention of Terrorism Act provide the police with special powers to obtain information needed in connection with terrorist investigations, including investigations into terrorist finances. The powers apply where a terrorist investigation is in progress and the material concerned will be of substantial value to that investigation. The main powers (and those most likely to be of relevance to a financial investigation) are those which enable the police in England, Wales or Northern Ireland:

(i)   to apply to a justice of the peace for a search warrant in respect of material which does not include excluded or special procedure material or material subject to legal privilege (as defined by sections 10 to 14 of PACE);

(ii)   to apply to a circuit judge for a production order in respect of excluded or special procedure material. A production order will require the holder of the material in question to hand it over to the police or to give them access to it within a specified period;

(iii)   to apply to a circuit judge for a search warrant in relation to excluded or special procedure material. This power may only be used where a production order has been made and not been complied with, or where the making of a production order would be impracticable or inappropriate.

15.8   These powers are backed by a provision enabling the police to apply to a circuit judge for an explanation order. This is an order requiring any specified person to provide an explanation of material obtained by means of a search warrant or production order under Schedule 7. The provision makes it an offence to give false or misleading information in response to such an order.

15.9   Similar provisions for Scotland are also set out in Schedule 7.

Tipping off

15.10   The investigative powers are also backed by a "tipping off" offence in section 17 of the Prevention of Terrorism Act (as amended by section 50 of the Criminal Justice Act 1993). This provision makes it unlawful to make a disclosure likely to be prejudicial to a terrorist investigation, or to interfere with material likely to be of assistance to an investigation.

(ii)   *Confiscation*

15.11   Until their repeal in August 1996, sections 47 to 52 and Schedule 4 to the Northern Ireland (Emergency Provisions) Act 1991 (as amended by Part IV of the Criminal Justice Act 1993) contained provisions for the confiscation of the proceeds of terrorist related activities. These provisions were only available in Northern Ireland.

15.12   However, a separate, terrorist-related confiscation scheme is no longer necessary given the enactment of the Proceeds of Crime (Northern Ireland) Order 1996. This makes provision in Northern Ireland for the confiscation of the proceeds of all serious crime, broadly comparable to that in England and Wales, and also creates additional powers of investigation which are not generally available elsewhere in the United Kingdom. Further details are given in Chapter 20.

SECTION 5
THE FORFEITURE OF DRUG TRAFFICKING CASH

16

The forfeiture of drug trafficking cash

16.1   Part II of the Drug Trafficking Act 1994 contains important powers enabling the police and Customs to obtain the forfeiture of drug trafficking cash. The powers apply to cash which is being imported into or exported from the United Kingdom including cash being brought to any place in the United Kingdom for the purpose of export, and they are available throughout the United Kingdom. For the purposes of Part II "cash" includes coins and notes in any currency.

16.2   The main characteristics of the provisions are:

- cash may be forfeited which represents the proceeds of drug trafficking or is intended for use in drug trafficking;

- the drug trafficking cash may be forfeited without any need for a criminal conviction;

- it is only necessary to prove on the balance of probabilities that the cash is drug trafficking cash;

- the forfeiture order is made by the magistrates' court.

16.3   Part II of the Drug Trafficking Act should be read in conjunction with the Magistrates' Courts (Detention and Forfeiture of Drug Trafficking Cash) Rules 1991 [S.I. 1991/1923], as amended by the Magistrates' Courts (Miscellaneous Amendments) Rules 1994 [S.I. 1994/3154 (L.20)], which set out the practical procedures to be followed in cases involving drug trafficking cash.

16.4   Drug trafficking cash may be seized and detained if it exceeds the prescribed sum (currently £10,000). This amount may be changed at any time by statutory instrument. Where the cash is in a currency other than sterling the prevailing exchange rate should be used to calculate whether the cash falls above or below the minimum amount.

Seizure

16.5   Part II of the Drug Trafficking Act envisages three possible stages in the forfeiture process, *seizure, detention and forfeiture*. It allows police and Customs to seize cash on import or export and detain it for an initial period of up to 48 hours, provided there are reasonable grounds for suspecting that the cash directly or indirectly represents any person's proceeds of drug trafficking, or is intended for use in drug trafficking.

First application for further detention

16.6   Seized cash cannot be detained for more than 48 hours without authority. Consequently, an application for authority to detain the cash further must be made within 48 hours of its seizure, and it is important to note that this period takes no account of Sundays or Bank Holidays. The cash may then be detained, on authorisation by a

Justice of the Peace, for an initial period of up to 3 months, renewable on application to a magistrates' court.

16.7 For a first application for further detention of the cash to succeed a Justice of the Peace must be satisfied on two counts:

- that there are reasonable grounds for suspecting that the cash directly or indirectly represents any person's proceeds of drug trafficking or is intended for use in drug trafficking; and

- the continued detention of the cash must be justified while its origin or derivation is investigated or consideration is given to the institution (whether in the United Kingdom or not) of criminal proceedings against any person for an offence with which the cash is connected.

16.8 A first application for the further detention of suspected drug trafficking cash should be made to a Justice of the Peace who ordinarily acts for the petty sessions area in which the cash was seized. The procedure for such applications is set out in the 1991 Rules. Application must be made in writing in the format prescribed by the Rules and a copy given to the person from whom the cash was seized.

16.9 Information given in the written application must be sworn on oath at the hearing. The applicant may also be required to answer questions under oath. Any statement in response by the person from whom the cash was seized may also be taken under oath. The Justice of the Peace must record any statements under oath which are not already recorded in the written application.

16.10 Most first time applications for the further detention of cash will be dealt with at the court house where the Justices' Clerk will be at hand to assist with the recording of statements and otherwise. The statute does, however, permit the hearing to take place away from the court house. There may exceptionally be circumstances where such a hearing is required.

16.11 Part II of the Drug Trafficking Act 1994 applies equally to cash which is not carried on the person. This includes cash contained in a letter, parcel or container. An officer seizing unattended cash would be expected to take reasonable steps to establish the owner, sender or intended recipient of the cash.

16.12 A Justice of the Peace may not, however, decline to hear an application solely on the grounds that the applicant is unable to prove that the sender or intended recipient of an unattended letter, parcel or container has received a copy of the written application.

16.13 The Justice's order for a first period of continued detention of the cash must be made in the form prescribed by the Rules. Notice of the Justice's order must be given by the applicant to any person appearing to the applicant to be affected by it. Thereafter, it is the job of the court clerk to notify those people of any subsequent application for further detention, release or forfeiture of the cash.

16.14 Unless it is required as evidence of an offence, cash detained for more than 48 hours must be placed in an interest bearing account and the interest must be paid with the cash when it is forfeited or released.

Second and subsequent application for further detention

16.15 A second and subsequent application for further detention of the cash must be made to a magistrates' court and must be made on the form prescribed by the 1991 Rules. Further periods of detention of up to 3 months at a time may be authorised by a magistrates' court up to a total of 2 years from the date on which a Justice of the Peace first orders the continued detention of the cash.

16.16   At the end of the 2 year period the cash must be released unless:

- application is made within the 2 year period to a magistrates' court for forfeiture of the cash; or

- criminal proceedings are instituted within the 2 year period (in the United Kingdom or elsewhere) against any person for an offence with which the cash is connected.

If either of these applies, the cash cannot be released until the proceedings for the forfeiture of the cash or the proceedings for the offence have been concluded.

Release

16.17   Detained cash may be released at any time by a magistrates' court, police or Customs officer if its continued detention is no longer justified. A police or Customs officer may release the cash without application to the court, but must first notify the Justice of the Peace or magistrates' court under whose order the cash is being detained.

16.18   Where the person from whom the cash was seized, or on whose behalf it was being imported or exported, wants the cash released, application must be made to a magistrates' court. Any direction made by the magistrates' court for release of the cash should be in the format prescribed by the Rules and should provide for the release of the cash within 7 days of the making of the direction or such later date as may be agreed with the person from whom the cash was seized.

16.19   Thus, with the agreement of the person from whom the cash was seized, provision may be made to avoid loss of interest where cash is deposited with a bank on 7-day notice and the direction for release is made during a weekend or bank holiday.

Forfeiture

16.20   Section 43 of the Drug Trafficking Act enables the magistrates' court to order the forfeiture of the cash. An application for forfeiture should be addressed to the Clerk to the Justices for the petty sessions area in which the seizure was made.

16.21   Any person to whom notice of the application has been given may attend the hearing and be heard on the question of whether a forfeiture order should be made. The fact that such a person does not attend shall not, however, prevent the court from hearing the application.

16.22   Forfeited cash plus accrued interest is paid into the Consolidated Fund, but only after any appeal against forfeiture has been determined or otherwise disposed of. In any other case the cash may not be paid into the Consolidated Fund until the statutory appeal period (30 days) has elapsed.

16.23   HM Customs, which deals with most cases under Part II of the Drug Trafficking Act, has established standard procedures for the handling of detained and forfeited cash. Further details may be obtained from:

Accounting Services Division,
HM Customs & Excise,
7th Floor Central,
Alexander House,
21 Victoria Avenue,
Southend-on-Sea,
Essex,
SS2 6AB.

Appeals

16.24   An appeal against the decision of a magistrates' court to order the forfeiture of drug trafficking cash lies to the Divisional Court on a point of law. In addition, section 44 of the Drug Trafficking Act provides for an appeal to the Crown Court by way of a rehearing. This provision applies only to forfeiture orders made under the Act, on or after 3 February 1995, and not to orders made under the unconsolidated provision in the Criminal Justice (International Co-operation) Act 1990: see Schedule 2, paragraph 7 to the Drug Trafficking Act.

16.25   A magistrates' court may order forfeited cash to be released to enable the appellant to meet his or her legal expenses in connection with the appeal. If the appeal is upheld the forfeited cash, or the amount of it left where cash has been released for legal expenses, may be released, together with any accrued interest. New rules of court, the Magistrates' Courts (Miscellaneous Amendments) Rules 1994 [S.I. 1994/3154(L.20] have been brought forward to deal with the release of cash for legal expenses.

SECTION 6
MONEY LAUNDERING

17
Background

17.1   Money laundering is the process by which the proceeds of crime are converted into assets which appear to have a legitimate origin, so that they can be retained permanently or recycled into further criminal enterprises.

17.2   If the proceeds of crime are allowed to be lodged unhindered in financial institutions, criminals can at first gain influence over the institutions and finally control them. Where criminal proceeds are used to buy and operate legitimate businesses, competitors find themselves unable to compete and are driven out of business. Unchecked, money laundering can destabilise financial institutions, financial sectors and, in certain cases, entire economies.

17.3   Widespread concern about the threat of money laundering and drug money laundering in particular has led to a number of recent international initiatives. The 1988 UN Drugs Convention requires parties to criminalise drug money laundering. The Financial Action Task Force (FATF) was set up at the July 1989 G7 Summit specifically to develop and promote policies to combat money laundering. The 1990 Council of Europe Confiscation Convention requires parties to criminalise certain money laundering activities. The EC Money Laundering Directive of June 1991 (91/308/EEC) requires EC member states to prevent the use of their financial systems for money laundering.

17.4   Countries can take three main steps to combat money laundering:

● they can criminalise it;

● they can take measures to identify laundered proceeds in financial institutions and elsewhere, with a view to their confiscation;

● they can pass laws and establish systems to prevent the proceeds of crime being laundered in the first place.

The United Kingdom has taken all three steps. Its money laundering offences are described in Chapter 18.

17.5   As far as the second step is concerned, United Kingdom money laundering legislation requires the employees of financial institutions and others to disclose suspicious transactions to the authorities. One of the purposes of the legislation is to identify criminal assets so that they can be confiscated. Very broad immunities against civil action are built into the legislation to protect people who disclose suspicions of money laundering to the authorities.

17.6   Under the terms of the legislation, a suspicion or belief of money laundering can be disclosed to any police or Customs officer. Where a person is in employment, however, the suspicion or belief can be disclosed instead to the person nominated within the organisation to receive such disclosures and pass them to the authorities. Under the Money Laundering Regulations 1993, persons and organisations carrying on relevant financial business within the meaning of the Regulations are required to nominate such a person, known as a Money Laundering Reporting Officer (MLRO).

17.7   In practice the financial institutions pass suspicious transaction reports not to local constables or Customs officers but to the National Criminal Intelligence Service (NCIS) in London. Having evaluated a disclosure, NCIS will distribute it as appropriate to police forces or HM Customs for further action.

17.8   As far as the third step against money laundering is concerned, much effort has been put into preventing the proceeds of crime from entering the financial system. The Money Laundering Regulations 1993 [S.I. 1993/1933] require the financial and professional services sector to introduce systems and controls to prevent money laundering. These requirements are backed up with criminal sanctions for failure to comply. In particular, institutions must ensure that:

- proper identification is obtained from customers;

- records are kept of identification produced and of transactions made;

- a person is nominated within the organisation to receive suspicions of money laundering from staff and pass them to the authorities;

- staff are trained from time to time to guard against money laundering.

17.9   Another initiative was the publication, in December 1990, of Money Laundering Guidance Notes for Banks and Building Societies drawn up in consultation between the British Bankers' Association, the Building Societies Association and the law enforcement authorities. Similar Guidance Notes for Insurance Business and Investment Business were published in July and September 1991 respectively.

17.10   The Money Laundering Guidance Notes were revised in 1993. Copies may be purchased from:

The British Bankers Association,
10 Lombard Street,
London, EC3V 9EL.

18
Legislation

Offences

18.1   As with the confiscation legislation, the United Kingdom has drug money laundering laws, crime money laundering laws and terrorist money laundering laws. Following the entry into force of the Criminal Justice Act 1993, the law as it relates to drug and crime money laundering is much the same. Consequently, this chapter deals with them together.

18.2   This chapter describes the money laundering legislation of England and Wales. Scotland and Northern Ireland have similar provisions in place. In England and Wales, the drug money laundering offences catch the laundering of the proceeds of drug trafficking as defined in the Drug Trafficking Act 1994.

18.3   The crime money laundering offences are targeted against the laundering of the proceeds of offences to which Part VI of the Criminal Justice Act 1988 applies: that is to say, the proceeds of the summary offences specified in Schedule 4 to the 1988 Act and of all indictable offences, **apart from drug trafficking offences and terrorist offences under Part III of the Prevention of Terrorism (Temporary Provisions) Act 1989**.

18.4   For the purposes of these drug and crime money laundering offences it does not matter that the conduct which generated the laundered proceeds may have taken place abroad, provided that the actual laundering took place in England and Wales (or, as the case may be, Scotland or Northern Ireland). It is not necessary for the conduct which gave rise to the proceeds to be an offence in the country where it took place.

Laundering another person's proceeds

18.5   This chapter first describes the offences which may be committed where one launders another person's proceeds.

Assisting another to retain the proceeds of crime

18.6   This offence is contained in section 50 of the Drug Trafficking Act 1994 and section 93A of the Criminal Justice Act 1988. Broadly, the activities which may constitute the offence are:

- assisting a person to retain or control the proceeds of drug trafficking/other crime;

- using a person's proceeds of drug trafficking/other crime to place funds at his/her disposal;

- using a person's proceeds of drug trafficking/other crime to acquire property by way of investment for his/her benefit.

18.7   To commit the offence, one must **know or suspect** that the person is or has been engaged in drug trafficking/other crime, or has benefited from it.

Acquiring, possessing or using another's proceeds of crime

18.8   This offence is contained in section 51 of the Drug Trafficking Act 1994 and section 93B of the Criminal Justice Act 1988. The activities which may constitute the offence are:

- acquiring, possessing or using another person's proceeds of drug trafficking/other crime.

To commit the offence, one must **know** that the property is, or in whole or in part directly or indirectly represents, that person's proceeds of drug trafficking/other crime.

18.9   The offence only applies where the launderer acquires, possesses or uses the property for inadequate "consideration". In other words, if one pays full value for the property, one does not commit the offence. However, the provision of goods or services which are of assistance in criminal conduct is not regarded as consideration.

Concealing etc another person's proceeds of crime

18.10   This offence is contained in section 49 of the Drug Trafficking Act 1994 and section 93C of the Criminal Justice Act 1988.

18.11   The activities which may constitute the offence are:

- concealing or disguising property;

- converting or transferring property or removing it from the jurisdiction (meaning England and Wales in this context).

To commit the offence one must **know or have reasonable grounds to suspect** that the property in question is, or in whole or in part directly or indirectly represents, another person's proceeds of drug trafficking/other crime. One must also carry out these activities for the purpose of assisting somebody to avoid prosecution for a relevant offence or the making or enforcement of a confiscation order against him/her.

18.12   It will be noted that this offence, unlike the other two described above, may be committed where one had *reasonable grounds to suspect* that the property came from crime. In other words, it is not necessary for the prosecution to prove that the person laundering the property actually did suspect that it came from crime, only that he or she *should have suspected* that it did. It is, however, necessary to prove that the laundering was carried out for one of the purposes described above (avoidance of prosecution or making or enforcement of a confiscation order).

Laundering one's own proceeds

18.13   This offence is contained in section 49 of the Drug Trafficking Act 1994 and section 93C of the Criminal Justice Act 1988.

18.14   The activities which may constitute the offence are the same as those mentioned in paragraph 18.11. For the offence to be committed, the property must be, or in whole or in part directly or indirectly represent, one's own proceeds of drug trafficking/other crime. One must conceal, disguise, convert, transfer or remove the property from the jurisdiction for the purpose of avoiding one's own prosecution for a relevant offence or the making or enforcement of a confiscation order against oneself.

Penalties

18.15   The maximum penalty for all the money laundering offences described above is fourteen years imprisonment and an unlimited fine on indictment, and six months imprisonment and a fine not exceeding the statutory maximum (currently £5,000) on summary conviction.

Failure to disclose knowledge or suspicion of money laundering

18.16   This offence is contained in section 52 of the Drug Trafficking Act 1994. It may be committed where:

- information or some other matter came to one's attention in the course of one's trade, profession, business or employment; and

- as a result of it one knows or suspects that another person is engaged in drug money laundering; and

- one fails to disclose the information or other matter concerned to the police or Customs (or "up the line" to the person nominated by one's employer to receive such disclosures and pass them to the authorities).

18.17.   This offence applies only where there is knowledge or suspicion that another person is engaged in *drug* money laundering. There is also an offence of failure to disclose a knowledge or suspicion that another person is providing financial assistance for terrorism - see the concluding paragraphs of this chapter on terrorist money laundering.

18.18   The offence described in paragraph 18.16 is not committed where a professional legal adviser fails to disclose any information or other matter which has come to him or her in privileged circumstances. No information or other matter is to be treated as coming to a legal adviser *in privileged circumstances* if it is communicated or given with a view to furthering a criminal purpose.

Tipping-off offences

18.19   These offences are contained in section 53 and 58 of the Drug Trafficking Act 1994 and section 93D of the Criminal Justice Act 1988.

Tip-off in connection with money laundering investigation

18.20   This offence is contained in section 53(1) of the Drug Trafficking Act 1994 and section 93D(1) of the Criminal Justice Act 1988. It may be committed where:

- one knows or suspects that a police or Customs officer is acting or proposing to act in connection with an investigation being conducted or about to be conducted into money laundering; and

- one discloses information or any other matter likely to prejudice the investigation (or proposed investigation).

Tip-off in connection with disclosure

18.21   This offence is contained in section 53(2) and (3) of the Drug Trafficking Act 1994 and section 93D(2) and (3) of the Criminal Justice Act 1988. It may be committed where:

- one knows or suspects that a suspicious transaction, or suspicion that another person is engaged in drug money laundering has been disclosed to a police or Customs officer; and

• one passes on information or any other matter likely to prejudice any investigation which might be made following the disclosure.

Section 53(3) of the Drug Trafficking Act 1994 and section 93D(3) of the Criminal Justice Act 1988 make it clear that the offence is also committed where the disclosure to which the tip-off relates is made "up the line" to the person nominated by an employer to receive such disclosures and pass them to the authorities.

Tip-off in connection with production order or warrant

18.22   This offence, which applies only in drug cases, is contained in section 58 of the Drug Trafficking Act 1994. The offence may be committed where:

• a production order under section 55 of the Act has been made or applied for and not refused; or

• a warrant under section 56 of the Act has been issued; and

• one knows or suspects the investigation is taking place and one makes any disclosure likely to prejudice it.

18.23   The tipping-off offences attract the same safeguards covering the disclosure of information or other matters subject to legal privilege as those described in paragraph 18.18 above.

Penalties

18.24   The maximum penalty for the offence of failing to disclose a knowledge or suspicion that another is engaged in drug money laundering, and for all the tipping-off offences, is five years imprisonment and an unlimited fine on indictment. The maximum penalty for all these offences on summary conviction is six months imprisonment and a fine not exceeding the statutory maximum.

Failure to install and maintain anti-money laundering systems

18.25   The Money Laundering Regulations 1993 [S.I.1993/1933] require financial institutions to put in place systems to deter money laundering and to assist the authorities to detect money laundering activities. The Regulations apply to:

• all banks, building societies and other credit institutions;

• all individuals and firms authorised to conduct investment business under the Financial Services Act 1986;

• all insurance companies covered by the EC Life Directives, including the life business of Lloyd's of London;

• all other undertakings carrying out any of the range of financial activities listed in the annex to the Second Banking Supervision Directive [89/646/EEC, SI 1992/3218]. This includes notably bureaux de change and money transmission services.

18.26   The Money Laundering Regulations 1993 also establish criminal offences for those who fail to ensure that adequate systems are put into place and maintained. The offences are contained in Regulation 5 (read with Regulation 6) of the 1993 Regulations.

18.27   The offences may be committed where a person to whom the Regulations apply (including a body corporate) forms a business relationship or carries out a one-off transaction in the course of relevant financial business without:

- maintaining identification, record-keeping, or internal reporting procedures in accordance with the Regulations, or such other procedures of internal control and communication as may be necessary to forestall and prevent money laundering;

- taking appropriate measures from time to time to make employees who handle relevant financial business aware of those procedures and the money laundering statutes;

- providing such employees with training from time to time in the recognition and handling of transactions which may be money laundering.

18.28   Regulation 6 makes it clear that where an offence is committed by a body corporate, partnership or unincorporated association, directors and managers of those bodies and certain other specified persons may be guilty of the offence.

Penalties

18.29   The maximum penalty for a contravention of Regulation 5 of the Money Laundering Regulations 1993 is two years imprisonment and an unlimited fine on indictment and a fine not exceeding the statutory maximum on summary conviction.

Terrorist funds

18.30   Offences and disclosure provisions in relation to the laundering of terrorist funds are contained in the Prevention of Terrorism (Temporary Provisions) Act 1989.

18.31   The Prevention of Terrorism (Temporary Provisions) Act 1989 created, in section 11, an offence of assisting in the retention or control of terrorist funds, and in section 12 a disclosure scheme under which suspicious transactions are reported to the National Criminal Intelligence Service.

18.32   In the Criminal Justice Act 1993, the terrorist money laundering provisions in the 1989 Act were amended in similar fashion to the drug and all crime money laundering legislation.

18.33   For example, the 1993 Act created a provision for disclosures to be made to a workplace supervisor, as well as direct to the police. The 1993 Act also created new offences of failure to disclose knowledge or suspicion of terrorist money laundering activity similar to the new offence of failure to disclose knowledge or suspicion that another is engaged in drug money laundering.

SECTION 7
SCOTTISH AND NORTHERN IRISH
PROVISIONS

19
Scottish provisions

Drug trafficking

19.1   In most fundamental respects, the Scottish drug trafficking confiscation scheme resembles that of England and Wales. A confiscation order under the Scottish legislation is also an order to pay an amount of money, expressed in sterling.

19.2   Confiscation of the proceeds of drug trafficking following a conviction for a drug trafficking offence was introduced by the Criminal Justice (Scotland) Act 1987 (Chapter 41). A number of amendments to this legislation were contained in the Criminal Justice (Scotland) Act 1995 (Chapter 20), which also introduced a confiscation regime in Scotland for proceeds of general crime.

19.3   Provisions of both Acts have recently been consolidated in the Proceeds of Crime (Scotland) Act 1995 (Chapter 43) which came into force on 1 April 1996 and repealed the chapters dealing with drug trafficking offences in the Criminal Justice (Scotland) Act 1987 and the Criminal Justice (Scotland) Act 1995. However, the drug trafficking production order powers in the 1987 Act have been consolidated in the Criminal Law (Consolidation) (Scotland) Act 1995, Part V.

19.4   The Proceeds of Crime (Scotland) Act 1995 thus contains Scotland's scheme for both drug trafficking and all crime confiscation. The provision in the Act reflects the separate system of criminal law and procedure which applies in Scotland. Recent amendments to the drug trafficking scheme brought the Scottish legislation more closely into line with the Drug Trafficking Act 1994. However, notwithstanding the recent amendments, Scottish confiscation legislation continues to differ in some respects from its counterpart in England and Wales.

19.5   The High Court of Justiciary or sheriff court in Scotland or, in certain circumstances the sheriff court sitting summarily, may consider confiscation on the prosecutor's motion, but is under no statutory obligation to do so. The court may make certain assumptions when determining whether an accused has benefited from the commission of an offence. When determining the amount of benefit derived from a drug trafficking offence the court may assume that any property held by the accused at any time since his conviction or any property transferred to the accused within 6 years prior to being indicted or served with a complaint may be held to represent proceeds of drug trafficking offences.

19.6   When determining the amount of benefit derived from other crime the court may assume that any property or economic advantage obtained since the commission of the offence and any expenditure of the accused since that date represent proceeds of crime.

19.7   In certain cases, ie. where there is a previous conviction for a relevant offence, or where there are two or more offences before the court, the court may assume that any property or economic advantage obtained by the accused within the last six years was obtained with the proceeds of crime. The accused may show, on a balance of probabilities, that the assumptions made by the court are not correct. The court has a discretion as to the amount of any confiscation order.

19.8   The court may make a restraint order. Restraint orders cannot be made earlier than 28 days before criminal proceedings are expected to be instituted (the legislation in England and Wales contains no similar procedure). Following conviction, the court may recall or vary a confiscation order within six years of the date of conviction for the offence from which the accused has benefited if further assets have been discovered. Similarly, where no confiscation order has been made and proceeds of crime are subsequently discovered, the court may make a confiscation order within six years of conviction.

19.9   There are, of course, differences between the ancillary provisions in the legislation of England and Wales and of Scotland which arise out of the separate development of the legal systems in the two jurisdictions. Charging orders, for example, are unknown in Scotland so there is no provision in the Proceeds of Crime (Scotland) Act 1995 to place a charge on property in connection with proceeds of drug trafficking or other crime in Scotland. Nor is there provision to enforce charging orders made in England and Wales in Scotland.

19.10   Similarly, the position of receiver does not exist in Scottish law so, when Scotland's first confiscation legislation was drafted (in the Criminal Justice (Scotland) Act 1987), it was necessary to establish a position, referred to in the Act as an *administrator*, to carry out the functions in Scotland exercised by receivers under the confiscation legislation in England and Wales.

19.11   Confiscation orders made in England and Wales under the Criminal Justice Act 1988 and the Drug Trafficking Act 1994 are enforceable in Scotland under sections 35 and 36 of the Proceeds of Crime (Scotland) Act 1995. Scottish drug trafficking confiscation orders are enforceable in England and Wales under an Order in Council, the Drug Trafficking Offences (Enforcement in England and Wales) Order 1988 [S.I. 1988/593].

Contact point

19.12   A contact point for restraint and confisction matters in Scotland is:

Fraud and Specialist Services Unit,
Crown Office,
25 Chambers Street,
Edinburgh,
EH1 1LA (FAX 0131 226 6861).

20
Northern Irish Provisions

20.1   The Proceeds of Crime (Northern Ireland) Order 1996 provides for the confiscation by the Northern Ireland courts of the proceeds of drug trafficking and other serious crime. The Order updates and restates the Criminal Justice (Confiscation) (Northern Ireland) Order 1990, which combined and adapted for Northern Ireland the confiscation provisions of both the Drug Trafficking Offences Act 1986 and Part VI of the Criminal Justice Act 1988.

20.2   The 1996 Order, which came into operation on 25 August 1996, reflects changes in the law of England and Wales up to and including those in the Drug Trafficking Act 1994 and the Proceeds of Crime Act 1995, both described in detail above. The 1996 Order also includes additional investigation powers which are not generally available elsewhere in the United Kingdom.

Confiscation orders

20.3   The powers of the Northern Ireland courts to make confiscation orders are broadly comparable to those currently available in England and Wales. The main confiscation provisions are contained in Articles 8 and 9 of the 1996 Order. These relate mainly to the Crown Court which, as in the corresponding England and Wales legislation, is required to go through the confiscation procedures whenever a defendant is convicted of an offence to which the Order applies and the prosecutor asks it so to proceed. The court also has the discretion to proceed of its own volition.

20.4   As in the corresponding England and Wales legislation, magistrates' courts may make a confiscation order only in respect of the limited range of highly profitable summary offences listed in Schedule 1 to the Order.

20.5   The 1996 Order also makes provision, as in England and Wales, for the court to reconsider making a confiscation order in a case where it did not previously do so, and to revise its original assessment of an offender's proceeds from criminal conduct, within six years of the original conviction. These powers are contained in Articles 17, 18 and 19 of the 1996 Order.

20.6   Article 24 of the 1996 Order gives the High Court power to make a confiscation order against the estate of a convicted criminal who has died, or against a defendant who has absconded. This power differs from that in England and Wales, where it only applies to drug trafficking offences, whereas in Northern Ireland it exists in respect of all offences to which the 1996 Order applies.

20.7   Northern Ireland confiscation orders are enforceable in England and Wales under the Drug Trafficking Act 1994 (Enforcement of Northern Ireland Confiscation Orders) Order 1995 [S.I. 1995/1967] and the Criminal Justice Act 1988 (Enforcement of Northern Ireland Confiscation Orders) Order 1995 [S.I. 1995/1968]. There is similar legislation in place for the enforcement of England and Wales confiscation orders in Northern Ireland.

Investigative powers

20.8   Article 49 of the 1996 Order creates an additional power of investigation, which may be used in relation to investigations into whether any person has benefited from criminal conduct or into the extent or whereabouts of the proceeds of criminal conduct. Article 49 provides for a county court judge to appoint a person other than a constable to assist the RUC with such investigations. Such a person is known as a financial investigator and has powers which are set out in Schedule 2 to the Order.

20.9   A financial investigator may require any person whom he/she believes has information relevant to the investigation to attend to answer questions, to produce documents or to provide information in writing. Answers given to a financial investigator are not normally admissible in evidence. Failure to comply with a requirement made by a financial investigator is an offence punishable by up to 5 years' imprisonment.

20.10   The powers of the financial investigator are similar to those of the Director of the Serious Fraud Office and of an authorised investigator who would have been appointed under section 57 of the Northern Ireland (Emergency Provisions) Act 1991 prior to its repeal. Unlike the authorised investigator, however, the financial investigator's powers may only be exercised in Northern Ireland.

Contact Point

20.11   The Director of Public Prosecutions for Northern Ireland has established a Restraint and Confiscation Section which is responsible for dealing with restraint and confiscation matters in that jurisdiction. It is:

Restraint and Confiscation Section,
Department of the Director of Public Prosecutions for Northern Ireland,
Royal Courts of Justice,
Chichester Street,
Belfast BT1 3NX (FAX 01232 546111).

PART 2
THE INTERNATIONAL
DIMENSION

SECTION 8
INTERNATIONAL CONFISCATIONS

21
First principles

21.1   Nowadays much major acquisitive crime has an international element. This section explains how the proceeds of drug trafficking and other serious crime may be confiscated across national boundaries.

Designation

21.2   Under its laws, the United Kingdom can only offer assistance in freezing and confiscating the proceeds of drug trafficking and other serious crime to countries which have been **designated** for the purpose. Countries are designated separately for drug trafficking confiscation assistance and all crime confiscation assistance (excluding drug trafficking).

21.3   Countries are designated where the United Kingdom has an expectation of reciprocal confiscation assistance. Other countries provide reciprocal confiscation assistance where a confiscation convention, treaty, agreement or other relevant international instrument on confiscation is in force between them and the United Kingdom. Consequently, countries are designated where they ratify an international confiscation instrument to which the United Kingdom is a party, or the United Kingdom concludes a bilateral agreement with a country.

21.4   Countries are only designated once for drug trafficking or all crime confiscation assistance. There may, however, be more than one relevant international confiscation instrument in force between them and the United Kingdom. For example, Italy has been designated for drug trafficking confiscation assistance, but there are two multilateral conventions and a bilateral agreement in force between this country and Italy, all of which require the parties to provide one another with assistance in drug trafficking confiscation matters.

21.5   In England and Wales, countries are designated for drug trafficking confiscation assistance in an Order in Council, the Drug Trafficking Offences Act 1986 (Designated Countries and Territories) Order 1990 and its subsequent amendment Orders. Details of these Orders are given in Annex A. Despite the repeal of the 1986 Act, this Order in Council remains in force. **It is important to note, however, that at the time of writing a new Order in Council under the Drug Trafficking Act 1994, the Drug Trafficking Act 1994 (Designated Countries and Territories) Order 1996 [S.I. 1996/2880] has been laid before Parliament. It is expected to replace the old Order under the 1986 Act with effect from 1 January 1997.** The new Order should be easier for enforcement authorities to use than its predecessors as it redesignates for the purposes of the 1994 Act the countries and territories previously designated in several statutory instruments, as well as designating certain countries and territories for the first time. The 1990 Order in Council will, broadly speaking, continue to apply to old cases started before the new Order comes into force.

21.6   The 1990 Order in Council under the Drug Trafficking Offences Act 1986 contains the law as it relates to the enforcement in England and Wales of foreign drug trafficking confiscation orders. Consequently, in order to find out about, for example, restraint in connection with the enforcement here of another country's drug trafficking confiscation order, it is necessary to consult this Order in Council, not the Drug Trafficking Act itself. Scotland and Northern Ireland operate a similar system.

21.7   The same applies to other countries' confiscation orders relating to other crimes. The legislation applicable to the enforcement of such confiscation orders in England and Wales is not Part VI of the Criminal Justice Act 1988 itself, but the *Criminal Justice Act 1988 (Designated Countries and Territories) Order 1991* and its subsequent amendment Orders. Again, details of these are given in Annex A.

21.8   Most countries in the world have now been designated for drug trafficking confiscation assistance. A small number of countries have been designated for all crime confiscation assistance. A list of designated countries with which there is a relevant international convention or agreement in force is given at Annexes B to D. Further countries which are expected to be in these categories shortly are also noted.

Central Authority

21.9   All incoming and outgoing requests for the restraint and confiscation of assets under international conventions and agreements must be made through the United Kingdom Central Authority in the Home Office. The United Kingdom Central Authority acts as the Central Authority for the whole of the United Kingdom, including Scotland and Northern Ireland, under confiscation conventions and agreements.

21.10   In addition to its responsibilities in confiscation cases, the United Kingdom processes international mutual legal assistance requests generally, where it acts on behalf of the Secretary of State for the Home Department under the Criminal Justice (International Co-operation) Act 1990. The United Kingdom Central Authority is responsible only for government to government assistance in criminal matters. It is not concerned with civil litigation. Its full address is:

> **The United Kingdom Central Authority for Mutual Legal Assistance in Criminal Matters,**
> **Judicial Cooperation Unit,**
> **Home Office,**
> **50 Queen Anne's Gate,**
> **London SW1H 9AT (FAX 0171-273-4400).**

21.11   The United Kingdom Central Authority has issued a booklet, "International Mutual Legal Assistance in Criminal Matters: United Kingdom Guidelines", which gives details of its role. Copies, available in English, French or Spanish, may be obtained by writing to the Central Authority at the above address.

The prosecutors' role

21.12   International confiscation requests are executed by CPS and Customs prosecutors and in both cases there is a specialised unit which oversees requests. In the case of the CPS it is:

> **Central Confiscation Branch,**
> **Crown Prosecution Service,**
> **50 Ludgate Hill,**
> **London, EC4M 7EX (FAX 0171 273 1325).**

In Customs cases it is:

Asset Forfeiture Unit,
Solicitor's Office,
HM Customs and Excise,
New King's Beam House,
22 Upper Ground,
London, SE1 9PJ (FAX 0171 865 5902).

21.13   In order to avoid unnecessary delays, and to reduce the work of the United Kingdom Central Authority and Central Authorities abroad, it is important that liaison should take place wherever necessary between the prosecutors in this country and the appropriate authorities abroad in preparing a request and supporting papers.

21.14   Once a request has been put out for action by the Central Authority here or abroad, the prosecutors in each country may maintain direct liaison with the appropriate authorities in the other country in dealing with any supplementary issues which may arise and do not require the attention of the Central Authority.

21.15   For example, where a United Kingdom confiscation order is sent abroad for enforcement, the prosecutor will need to monitor the progress that is being made in its enforcement, and the United Kingdom Central Authority should be informed when the enforcement process is complete.

21.16   In some cases involving incoming requests, it may be necessary to deal with the request, particularly a restraint request, very urgently. Under such circumstances, the request may, as appropriate, be copied to the CPS Central Confiscation Branch or the Customs Asset Forfeiture Unit, or to the Crown Office in Scotland or the Office of the Director of Public Prosecutions in Northern Ireland, at the same time as it is sent to the United Kingdom Central Authority.

22
Outgoing requests

Asset tracing

22.1   Some countries may be able to assist enforcement agencies here with asset tracing on an agency to agency basis. Furthermore, the 1988 UN Convention against Illicit Traffic in Narcotic Drugs and Psychotropic Substances ("the 1988 UN Drugs Convention") requires parties to assist one another, on a government to government basis, with asset tracing in drugs cases. The United Kingdom became a party to this Convention in 1991.

22.2   The 1990 Council of Europe Convention on Laundering, Search, Seizure and Confiscation of the Proceeds from Crime ("the Council of Europe Confiscation Convention") requires its parties to co-operate with each other to the widest extent possible for the purposes of investigations and proceedings aiming at the confiscation of proceeds and instrumentalities of drug trafficking and other serious crime.

22.3   The United Kingdom's bilateral confiscation agreements also provide a basis for submitting requests, on a government to government basis, for information and evidence for the purpose of an investigation or proceedings. Outgoing requests for assistance to the United Kingdom from overseas authorities, made on a government to government basis, should be channelled through the United Kingdom Central Authority described in Chapter 21.

Confiscation

22.4   When considering any outgoing request for the restraint or confiscation of assets, the person dealing with the case will need to ask:

Has the country been designated for the purpose to which the request relates?

For example, if the proposed request relates to a fraud, has the country in question been designated for all crime assistance? If not, there will be no all crime confiscation arrangements in force between that country and the United Kingdom, and the country in question will probably be unable to execute the request.

22.5   In theory, an outgoing restraint or confiscation request could be made to an undesignated country, but it might well be refused. Whilst designation is not a pre-requisite in legal terms for making a request, confiscation requests should normally be submitted only to countries which have been designated for the purpose to which the request relates. Any case where enforcement authorities wish to make a restraint or confiscation request to an undesignated country should be referred to the confiscation section in the Home Office for consideration. Its address is:

The Confiscation Section,
Judicial Co-operation Unit,
Organised and International Crime Directorate,
Home Office,
50 Queen Anne's Gate,
London SW1H 9AT (Fax 0171-273-4422).

22.6　　　If the country is designated, the next question is what material to submit with the request. To ascertain how the request is to be assembled, it is necessary to ask next:

What convention or agreement is in force between the United Kingdom and the country in question?

Annexes B to D show designated countries with which multilateral conventions and bilateral agreements are in force. Any case where it is desired to make a request to a country which has been designated for the necessary purpose, but where there appears to be no relevant convention or agreement in force, should be referred to the Confiscation Section in the Home Office for consideration.

22.7　　　Having established which convention or agreement is in force, its text will indicate what documentation should be submitted with the request.

The 1988 UN Drugs Convention

22.8　　　Most countries designated for drug trafficking confiscation assistance have been designated because they have ratified the 1988 UN Drugs Convention. Article 7 of the Convention requires the parties to assist one another in investigations and proceedings relating to drug trafficking. Article 5 of the Convention requires the parties to assist one another in tracing, freezing and confiscating the proceeds and instrumentalities of drug trafficking.

22.9　　　The material which should accompany a request for assistance under Article 5 of the 1988 Convention is set out in Article 7, paragraphs 6 to 19, of the Convention. Consequently, where an outgoing restraint or confiscation request is being considered in a drugs case, and the only instrument in force between the United Kingdom and the designated country is the 1988 Convention, the request should be drawn up in accordance with Article 5 and Article 7, paragraphs 6 to 19, of the Convention.

22.10　　　The Convention does not provide details of the authority in each country to which requests should be sent. These authorities are notified from time to time to the United Nations. The United Kingdom Central Authority has details of those authorities notified to date.

The Council of Europe Confiscation Convention

22.11　　　Unlike the 1988 UN Drugs Convention, the 1990 Council of Europe Convention on Laundering, Search, Seizure and Confiscation of the Proceeds from Crime is a specialist confiscation convention. It provides a comprehensive basis for multilateral co-operation in tracing, freezing and confiscating the proceeds and instrumentalities of all serious crime, including drug trafficking.

22.12　　　Consequently, it is possible to request assistance in drugs cases under both the 1988 and 1990 Conventions. All the countries which have ratified the 1990 Convention have also ratified the 1988 Convention. It is better to compile the request in accordance with the documentary requirements of the 1990 Convention because it is a specialist confiscation instrument. Furthermore, Article 7(6) of the 1988 Convention states that the provisions of that Article shall not affect states' obligations under any other treaty, bilateral or multilateral, which governs or will govern, in whole or in part, mutual legal assistance in criminal matters. However, there is no reason why both Conventions should not be referred to in the request.

22.13   Article 27 of the Council of Europe Confiscation Convention sets out the material which must be included in a request for assistance under the Convention. It applies whether the request concerns drug trafficking or any other crime.

22.14   Like the 1988 Convention, the 1990 Convention does not contain details of the authority in each country to which requests should be sent. These are notified from time to time to the Council of Europe. The United Kingdom Central Authority has details of the authorities notified to date.

Bilateral confiscation agreements

22.15   Since 1988 the United Kingdom has been concluding bilateral confiscation agreements and arrangements providing for co-operation in tracing, freezing and confiscating the proceeds and instrumentalities of drug trafficking and other serious crime.

22.16   Most of the agreements cover drug trafficking co-operation. Some cover drug trafficking and other serious crime. A list of agreements in force is at Annex D. Details of the agreements which have been published are given at Annex E.

22.17   The United Kingdom has concluded bilateral agreements with a number of countries which have ratified the 1988 and 1990 Conventions. Where a request is to be made to a country with which a bilateral agreement is in force the request should be drawn up under the terms of the agreement, regardless of whether there is also a multilateral convention in force relating to the same matters. The bilateral agreements provide the fullest details possible of both countries' practical requirements in the execution of confiscation requests.

22.18   The United Kingdom's bilateral agreements contain a number of provisions which are designed to assist practitioners in the compilation of a request. For example, they normally contain an article providing details of both countries' Central Authorities for the purposes of the agreement.

22.19   There will also be an article setting out what material must be included in a request under the agreement. This article should be read in conjunction with the further documentary requirements contained in the key articles on restraint and confiscation, which give details of the additional material which must be provided with restraint and confiscation requests.

22.20   Articles on language and authentication will state what language or languages the request must be drawn up in, and will provide details of any certification or authentication of documents that is required.

23
Incoming requests

Asset tracing

23.1   Production orders may be obtained in England and Wales by police and Customs under section 55 of the Drug Trafficking Act 1994 and section 93H of the Criminal Justice Act 1988 to assist investigations into drug trafficking and other acquisitive crimes which are being conducted abroad. Search warrants may be obtained under section 56 of the 1994 Act and section 93I of the 1988 Act for the same purpose. These powers may be exercised on behalf of overseas authorities, on an agency to agency basis, without the involvement of the United Kingdom Central Authority and without any need for a convention, treaty or agreement.

23.2   The United Kingdom may also offer assistance in tracing the proceeds of serious crime, on a government to government basis, in accordance with sections 4 and 7 of the Criminal Justice (International Co-operation) Act 1990. This assistance may also be provided to any other country without any need for a convention, treaty or agreement.

Confiscation

23.3   As explained in Chapter 21.5, the United Kingdom's powers to take action in respect of the proceeds of drug trafficking lodged in this country (or their value) in pursuit of a foreign confiscation order are contained in the Drug Trafficking Offences Act 1986 (Designated Countries and Territories) Order 1990 (to be replaced by a similar Order under the Drug Trafficking Act 1994), and its equivalents in Scotland and Northern Ireland. This chapter deals with the situation in England and Wales: see chapters 25 and 26 on the position in Scotland and Northern Ireland respectively.

23.4   The powers of the authorities in England and Wales to assist designated countries and territories in respect of the proceeds of crimes other than drug trafficking are contained in the Criminal Justice Act 1988 (Designated Countries and Territories) Order 1991. There are similar provisions in force in Northern Ireland.

23.5   England and Wales's 1990 and 1991 Orders in Council are based on the domestic drug trafficking and all crime confiscation legislation, modified to provide for the enforcement in England and Wales of external confiscation orders. The powers may only be brought to bear in connection with external confiscation orders made by a *court*. There is no provision for enforcing overseas administrative confiscation orders.

23.6   The main difference between the Orders in Council and the primary legislation is that the Orders in Council only need to provide for the *enforcement* of external orders, whereas the statutes enable domestic confiscation orders to be both made and enforced.

23.7   Once an external confiscation order has been made by a designated country it may be registered in the High Court and enforced in England and Wales. There is no role in international cases for the Crown Court, the magistrates' court or the county court.

23.8   Once it has authorised the registration of an external confiscation order, the High Court can appoint a receiver to realise it. The High Court also has the power to make a garnishee order as if the sum payable under the external confiscation order were due to the Crown under a High Court order or judgment. This is a useful way of confiscating monies in bank accounts in enforcement of an external confiscation order, without the need to appoint a receiver.

23.9   The Orders in Council permit most of the ancillary powers in the domestic confiscation legislation, such as pre-trial restraint, to be applied in England and Wales on behalf of designated countries. For example, a prosecutor from the Crown Prosecution Service or HM Customs and Excise may apply to the High Court for a restraint or charging order on behalf of the designated country when proceedings have been, or are about to be instituted in the designated country.

23.10   To assist the High Court in deciding whether proceedings have been or are about to be instituted abroad, the Orders in Council state the point at which proceedings are instituted under the law of a number of countries and territories. These are normally countries with which a bilateral confiscation agreement has been concluded.

23.11   The procedures to be followed in respect of proceedings in the High Court of England and Wales in connection with external confiscation orders are set out in Order 115 of the Rules of the Supreme Court 1965, which was inserted by S.I. 1986/2289 and has been amended a number of times since. Annex A contains further details.

Contents of incoming requests

23.12   It is very important that the material submitted to the High Court should contain all the information the court requires, and should be drawn up in a form which will enable the court to carry out the desired action without delay. This applies particularly to restraint requests, which may need to be executed with great urgency.

23.13   By their very nature, the multilateral confiscation conventions contain no information as to the material which the jurisdictions making up the United Kingdom require under their laws to execute a restraint or confiscation request. The following details may assist foreign authorities, and the United Kingdom authorities with which they will be liaising, to draft requests for the restraint and confiscation of property in England and Wales.

23.14   A letter of request signed by or on behalf of the Central Authority of a designated country should state the purpose of the request, including a description of the evidence, information or other assistance sought in connection with particular proceedings. Paragraphs 25.16 and 25.17 below list the information and other material which should accompany requests for the restraint and confiscation of assets.

23.15   For the purposes of paragraphs 25.16 and 25.17, a document will be considered to be "duly authenticated" only if it is certified by a person in his or her capacity as a judge, magistrate or officer of the relevant court in the designated country, or by or on behalf of the Central Authority of the designated country.

Restraint

23.16   A letter of request for the restraint of property should contain the following information:

(a)   personal details of the defendant - name, address, nationality, date of birth and present location;

(b)   details of the offence with which the defendant has been, or is about to be, charged or the civil action brought or about to be brought against the defendant in the designated country;

(c)   details of the law applicable to the charges and the evidence against the defendant;

(d)   particulars of the property which it is intended to restrain in the United Kingdom generally, and England and Wales in particular, and the persons holding it;

(e)   particulars of the link between the defendant and the property (very important if the property to be restrained is held in the name of a third party such as a company);

(f)   details of any court orders made in the designated country against the defendant in respect of his or her property, and brief general details of all property held by the defendant outside the United Kingdom.

A request for restraint should be accompanied by:

(a)   a *certificate* issued by or on behalf of the Central Authority of the designated country stating:

•   that proceedings have been instituted in the designated country and have not been concluded, or that proceedings are to be instituted in the designated country and, if so, when; and

•   (where no confiscation order has yet been made) that the confiscation order which it is expected the court in the designated country will make has the purpose of recovering property, or the value of property received in connection with drug trafficking or other serious crime; and

(b)   (where available) a *duly authenticated* copy of any court order made in the designated country against the defendant in respect of his or her property.

Confiscation

23.17.   A letter of request for the enforcement of a designated country's confiscation order should contain the following information:

(a)   personal details of the defendant - name, address, nationality, date of birth and present location;

(b)   particulars of all property held by the defendant in the United Kingdom, and England and Wales in particular;

(c)   details of any other party's interest in that property.

A request for the enforcement of a designated country's confiscation order should be accompanied by:

(a)   a copy of the confiscation order, *duly authenticated*;

(b)   a *certificate* issued by or on behalf of the Central Authority of the designated country stating:

•   that the designated country's confiscation order is in force and that neither the order nor any conviction to which it relates is subject to appeal;

•   that all or a certain amount of the sum payable under the order remains unpaid in the designated country or that other property recoverable under the order remains unrecovered there;

- that the confiscation order has the purpose of recovering property, or the value of property obtained in connection with drug trafficking or other serious crime;

- (where the person against whom the confiscation order was made did not appear in the confiscation proceedings) that he or she was notified of the proceedings in accordance with the law of the designated country in time to defend them.

Service of court orders on the defendant and other parties in the designated country

23.18.   The legislation of England and Wales requires that certain of its court orders, including restraint orders, should be served personally on the defendant and/or interested parties. This also applies where the orders have been obtained on behalf of another country. Such documents need to be channelled through the United Kingdom Central Authority to the Central Authority of the designated country, for service on the appropriate person(s) in the designated country.

23.19.   It is important that the completed memorandum of service is returned to the United Kingdom Central Authority quickly since delays could affect the High Court's willingness to continue the order. Countries are therefore asked to ensure wherever possible that the completed memorandum is returned to the United Kingdom Central Authority within a fortnight of despatch and that in the event of unavoidable delay an advance copy of the completed memorandum is sent to the United Kingdom Central Authority by FAX.

SECTION 9
ENFORCEMENT OF EXTERNAL
FORFEITURE ORDERS

24

The enforcement of external forfeiture orders

24.1   The forfeiture of the instrumentalities of crime falls outside the scope of this guide. The provisions relating to the enforcement of external forfeiture orders, however, are similar to those for enforcing external confiscation orders. Consequently, practitioners' attention is drawn to them here in brief.

24.2   Section 9 of the Criminal Justice (International Co-operation) Act 1990 applies throughout the United Kingdom. It enables Orders in Council to be made for the enforcement of external forfeiture orders. Each of the three constituent jurisdictions of the United Kingdom has its own principal Order in Council. In England and Wales it is the Criminal Justice (International Co-operation) Act 1990 (Enforcement of Overseas Forfeiture Orders) Order 1991 [S.I. 1991/1463] as amended. Further details of all the relevant Orders in Council are supplied in Annex A.

24.3   The Order in Council mentioned above provides for the enforcement in England and Wales of an order made by a court in a designated country for the forfeiture and destruction, or other disposal, of property used or intended to be used in connection with the commission of a drug trafficking offence or an indictable offence to which Part VI of the Criminal Justice Act 1988 applies.

24.4   The same designation system applies as with external confiscation orders. As with external confiscation orders, proceedings are in the High Court, where an external forfeiture order may be registered. Where an external forfeiture order is registered, the High Court may order the forfeiture of the property specified in the order. Third parties with an interest in the property are allowed to make representations to the court.

Terrorist funds

24.5   Schedule 4 to the Prevention of Terrorism (Temporary Provisions) Act 1989 contains a scheme to allow the enforcement in the United Kingdom of orders made in designated countries for the restraint or forfeiture of terrorist funds. The scheme applies to countries designated by Order in Council under the Act. One Order in Council has been made under the 1989 Act, designating India. It is the Prevention of Terrorism (Temporary Provisions) Act 1989 (Enforcement of External Orders) Order 1995 [S.I. 1995/760].

SECTION 10
SCOTTISH AND NORTHERN IRISH
PROVISIONS

25
Scottish provisions

25.1   Section 30 of the Criminal Justice (Scotland) Act 1987, which has been consolidated into sections 40 and 41 of the Proceeds of Crime (Scotland) Act 1995, enables a drug trafficking confiscation order made in a designated country or territory outside the United Kingdom to be registered in the Court of Session and enforced in Scotland. It also provides for certain powers, such as restraint, which are available domestically to be applied on behalf of designated countries and territories.

25.2   The provisions for enforcing external drug trafficking confiscation orders, therefore, are much the same as in England and Wales. The principal Scottish Order in Council is the Proceeds of Drug Trafficking (Designated Countries and Territories) (Scotland) Order 1991 [S.I. 1991/1467]. As with similar Orders in Council in England and Wales, this has been amended a number of times since, primarily to designate new countries and territories. Full details are to be found in Annex A. At the time of writing a new Order under the Proceeds of Crime (Scotland) Act 1995, covering both drug trafficking orders and orders for the confiscation of the proceeds of other crimes, is in preparation.

25.3   The United Kingdom Central Authority in the Home Office also acts as the Central Authority for Scotland under multilateral confiscation conventions and bilateral confiscation agreements. Where a request from a designated country or territory relates to Scotland, the Lord Advocate may act on the designated country's behalf in proceedings in the Court of Session in Scotland. A contact for confiscation work in Scotland is given in Chapter 19.12.

26
Northern Irish provisions

26.1   Article 27 of the Criminal Justice (Confiscation) (Northern Ireland) Order 1990 provides that the Secretary of State for Northern Ireland may, by order, apply provisions of the 1990 Order to confiscation orders made in countries designated under section 26 of the Drug Trafficking Offences Act 1986 and section 96 of the Criminal Justice Act 1988, and to proceedings which may result in such confiscation orders. Article 28 of the Criminal Justice (Confiscation) (Northern Ireland) Order 1990 provides for the registration in the High Court in Northern Ireland of confiscation orders made in designated countries.

26.2   The provisions for the enforcement of external confiscation orders are set out, for drugs, in the Criminal Justice (Confiscation) (Designated Countries and Territories) (Northern Ireland) Order 1991 [S.I. 1991/221] and, for other offences, in the Criminal Justice (Confiscation) (Designated Countries and Territories) (Northern Ireland) Order 1992 [S.I. 1992/198]. These Orders are amended from time to time to add new countries and make any other such amendments as may be necessary. Full details of the principal and amendment Orders are to be found in Annex A.

26.3   The United Kingdom Central Authority in the Home Office also acts as the Central Authority for Northern Ireland under multilateral confiscation conventions and bilateral confiscation agreements. Where a request from a designated country or territory relates to Northern Ireland, the Director of Public Prosecutions for Northern Ireland, the Crown Solicitor for Northern Ireland and the Commissioners of Customs and Excise may act on the designated country's behalf in proceedings in the High Court in Northern Ireland. A contact point for confiscation work in Northern Ireland is given in Chapter 20.11.

SECTION 11
DISPOSAL OF CONFISCATED ASSETS

27
The Seized Assets Fund

27.1   The government has decided that drug traffickers' assets confiscated under international agreements are to be spent on anti-drugs work. To this end the United Kingdom's Seized Assets Fund was established in April 1992 to provide the spending mechanism for these monies. Monies confiscated in domestic cases are not included in the scheme. Assets are considered to have been confiscated under an international agreement where:

- assets held by drug traffickers in the United Kingdom are confiscated here pursuant to a request from another country or territory under a bilateral confiscation agreement, the 1988 UN Drugs Convention or the 1990 Council of Europe Confiscation Convention; or

- assets held by drug traffickers abroad are confiscated and the country or territory where the confiscation takes place decides to share confiscated assets with the United Kingdom in recognition of the help provided by the British authorities in bringing the confiscation to fruition (see chapter 28).

27.2   The sums available for spending from the Seized Assets Fund will fluctuate considerably from year to year in line with receipts. A proportion of the monies in the Fund is set aside to finance a separate fund, the Central Drugs Fund, which the government has set up to meet the additional costs of international drug trafficking investigations. This fund is described in Home Office Circular 37/1990 (most recently updated in Home Office Circular 10/1994).

27.3   Spending from the Seized Assets Fund is for both enforcement and demand reduction projects. The Fund is not intended to support staff and other running costs. Among the projects on which money in the Fund has been spent are computers for HM Customs, encrypted radios for police and fast launches for anti-narcotics patrols by overseas customs services. Funding has also been provided for drug prevention, education and treatment projects.

28
International asset sharing

28.1   The country where a confiscation takes place has the right to the confiscated assets.   This also applies to assets confiscated under international agreements. Consequently, in an international operation the country originating a confiscation request can pay for the entire operation leading up to the final confiscation and yet have no access to the confiscated monies.

28.2   Countries have established international asset sharing to deal with this problem. The object of asset sharing is to ensure that confiscated monies are shared out fairly between the countries that have brought the confiscation to fruition. The country where the final confiscation has taken place may offer to share a portion of the confiscated monies with the other countries involved in the operation. The decision to share will take place spontaneously, or on request.

28.3   All confiscated drug proceeds shared with the United Kingdom are recycled into anti-drugs projects through the United Kingdom's Seized Assets Fund, described in Chapter 27. Consequently, the more foreign drug trafficking confiscation orders are enforced in the United Kingdom, and the more United Kingdom drug trafficking confiscation orders are enforced abroad, the more potential there is for spending through the Fund.

28.4   The Seized Assets Fund is also the mechanism through which the United Kingdom is able to share with other countries a proportion of the drug assets confiscated in this country under international agreements. In May 1992 the United Kingdom and the United States of America concluded a formal asset sharing arrangement, under which the United Kingdom has shared about £300,000 worth of assets confiscated in this country in execution of an American confiscation order in the case of the deceased Colombian drug trafficker Jose Rodriguez Gacha. The United Kingdom is able to share confiscated drug assets with any other country on a case by case basis.

ANNEX A
United Kingdom Confiscation Statutes and Statutory Instruments

Note: a number of these instruments have been repealed in part or in whole.

(a) Statutes and statutory instrument applicable throughout the United Kingdom

Prevention of Terrorism (Temporary Provisions) Act 1989 Chapter 4

Criminal Justice (International Co-operation) Act 1990 Chapter 5

Criminal Justice Act 1993 Chapter 36

Prevention of Terrorism (Temporary Provisions) Act 1989 (Enforcement of External Orders) Order 1995 [S.I. 1995/760].

(b) England and Wales

Statutes

Drug Trafficking Offences Act 1986 Chapter 32

Criminal Justice Act 1988 Chapter 33

Drug Trafficking Act 1994 Chapter 37

Proceeds of Crime Act 1995 Chapter 11

Statutory instruments

Orders in Council

Drug Trafficking Offences (Enforcement in England and Wales) Order 1988 [S.I. 1988/593]. Enforcement in England and Wales of Scottish drug trafficking confiscation orders.

Drug Trafficking Act 1994 (Enforcement of Northern Ireland Confiscation Orders) Order 1995 [S.I. 1995/1967]. Enforcement in England and Wales of Northern Ireland drug trafficking confiscation orders.

Criminal Justice Act 1988 (Enforcement of Northern Ireland Confiscation Orders) Order 1995 [S.I. 1995/1968]. Enforcement in England and Wales of Northern Ireland all crime confiscation orders.

Enforcement of external drug trafficking confiscation orders

Drug Trafficking Offences Act 1986 (Designated Countries and Territories) Order 1990 [S.I. 1990/1199].

Drug Trafficking Offences Act 1986 (Designated Countries and Territories) (Amendment) Order 1991 [S.I. 1991/1465].

Drug Trafficking Offences Act 1986 (Designated Countries and Territories) (Amendment) Order 1992 [S.I. 1992/1722].

Drug Trafficking Offences Act 1986 (Designated Countries and Territories) (Amendment) Order 1993 [S.I. 1993/1792].

Drug Trafficking Offences Act 1986 (Designated Countries and Territories) (Amendment) (No.2) Order 1993 [S.I. 1993/3158].

Drug Trafficking Offences Act 1986 (Designated Countries and Territories) (Amendment) Order 1994 [S.I. 1994/1641].

Note: at the time of writing, a new Order under the Drug Trafficking Act 1994, the Drug Trafficking Act 1994 (Designated Countries and Territories) Order 1996 [S.I. 1996/2880] has been laid before Parliament.

Addition of further offences to Schedule 4 to the Criminal Justice Act 1988

Criminal Justice Act 1988 (Confiscation Orders) Order 1990 [S.I. 1990/1570].

Criminal Justice Act 1988 (Confiscation Orders) Order 1995 [S.I. 1995/3145].

Criminal Justice Act 1988 (Confiscation Orders) Order 1996 [S.I. 1996/1716].

Enforcement of external all crime confiscation orders

Criminal Justice Act 1988 (Designated Countries and Territories) Order 1991 [S.I. 1991/2873].

Criminal Justice Act 1988 (Designated Countries and territories) (Amendment) Order 1993 [S.I. 1993/1790].

Criminal Justice Act 1988 (Designated Countries and Territories) (Amendment) (No.2) Order 1993 [S.I. 1993/3147].

Criminal Justice Act 1988 (Designated Countries and Territories) (Amendment) Order 1994 [S.I. 1994/1639].

Criminal Justice Act 1988 (Designated Countries and Territories) (Amendment) Order 1996 [S.I. 1996/278].

Note: at the time of writing, a new amendment Order, the Criminal Justice Act 1988 (Designated Countries and Territories and Territories) (Amendment) (No.2) Order 1996 [S.I. 1996/2877] has been laid before Parliament.

Minimum amount of drug trafficking cash for seizure, detention and forfeiture under Part II Drug Trafficking Act 1994

Criminal Justice (International Co-operation) Act 1990 (Detention and Forfeiture of Drug Trafficking Cash) Order 1991 [S.I. 1991/1816].

Enforcement of external forfeiture orders

Criminal Justice (International Co-operation) Act 1990 (Enforcement of Overseas Forfeiture Orders) Order 1991 [S.I. 1991/1463].

Criminal Justice (International Co-operation) Act 1990 (Enforcement of Overseas Forfeiture Orders) (Amendment) Order 1992 [S.I. 1992/1721].

Criminal Justice (International Co-operation) Act 1990 (Enforcement of Overseas Forfeiture Orders) (Amendment) Order 1993 [S.I. 1993/1791].

Criminal Justice (International Co-operation) Act 1990 (Enforcement of Overseas Forfeiture Orders) (Amendment) (No.2) Order 1993 [S.I. 1993/3148].

Criminal Justice (International Co-operation) Act 1990 (Enforcement of Overseas Forfeiture Orders) (Amendment) Order 1994 [S.I. 1994/1640].

Note: at the time of writing a new Order, the Criminal Justice (International Co-operation) Act 1990 (Enforcement of Overseas Forfeiture Orders) (Amendment) Order 1996 [S.I. 1996/2878] has been laid before Parliament.

Rules of Court

Crown Court Rules

Crown Court (Amendment) Rules 1986 [S.I. 1986/2151 (L. 17)]

Crown Court (Amendment) Rules 1989 [S.I. 1989/299]

Crown Court (Amendment) Rules 1991 [S.I. 1991/1288 (L. 13)]

Crown Court (Amendment) (No. 2) Rules 1994 [S.I. 1994/3153 (L. 19)]

Crown Court (Amendment) Rules 1995 [S.I. 1995/2618(L.9)]

Magistrates' Courts Rules

Magistrates' Courts (Amendment) Rules 1989 [S.I. 1989/300 (L. 4)]

Magistrates' Courts (Detention and Forfeiture of Drug Trafficking Cash) Rules 1991 [S.I. 1991/1923 (L. 30)]

Magistrates' Courts (Miscellaneous Amendments) Rules 1994 [S.I. 1994/3154 (L.20)]

Magistrates' Courts (Amendment) (No.2) Rules 1995 [S.I. 1995/2619(L.10)]

Supreme Court Rules

Order 115 of the Rules of the Supreme Court 1965 applies. Order 115 was added by R.S.C. (Amendment No.3) 1986 [S.I. 1986/2289] and has subsequently been amended by S.I. 1988/298, S.I. 1989/386, S.I. 1989/1307 and S.I. 1991/1884.

(c)   Scotland

Statutes

Criminal Justice (Scotland) Act 1987 Chapter 41

Criminal Justice (Scotland) Act 1995 Chapter 20

Proceeds of Crime (Scotland) Act 1995 Chapter 43

Orders under section 30 of the Criminal Justice (Scotland) Act 1987 (enforcement of external drug trafficking confiscation orders)

Confiscation of the Proceeds of Drug Trafficking (Designated Countries and Territories) (Scotland) Order 1991 [S.I. 1991/1467]

Confiscation of the Proceeds of Drug Trafficking (Designated Countries and Territories) (Scotland) Amendment Order 1992 [S.I. 1992/1733]

Confiscation of the Proceeds of Drug Trafficking (Designated Countries and Territories) (Scotland) Amendment Order 1993 [S.I. 1993/1806]

Confiscation of the Proceeds of Drug Trafficking (Designated Countries and Territories) (Scotland) Amendment (No.2) Order 1993 [S.I. 1993/3156]

Confiscation of the Proceeds of Drug Trafficking (Designated Countries and Territories) (Scotland) Amendment Order 1994 [S.I. 1994/1644]

Enforcement of external forfeiture orders

Criminal Justice (International Co-operation) Act 1990 (Enforcement of Overseas Forfeiture Orders) (Scotland) Order 1991 [S.I. 1991 1468]

Ditto, Amendment Order 1992 [S.I. 1992/1734]

Ditto, Amendment Order 1993 [S.I. 1993/1807]

Ditto, Amendment (No.2) Order 1993 [S.I. 1993 3155]

Ditto, Amendment Order 1994 [S.I. 1994/1645]

Rules of Court

In Scotland, Rules of Court apply generally; specific Rules applying to specific legislation are only made where it is considered essential. For the remainder of the proceedings, the general Rules of Court for criminal proceedings apply. The Act of Adjournal (Criminal Procedure) Rules 1996 [S.I. 1996/513] provide general Rules for criminal proceedings. The Rules of the Court of Session 1994 [S.I. 1994/1443] make specific provision for confiscation proceedings in Chapter 62, Part VII (Rules 62.47-54) and Chapter 76, Part I.

(d) Northern Ireland

Statutes

Northern Ireland (Emergency Provisions) Act 1991 Chapter 24

Orders under paragraph 1 of Schedule 1 to the Northern Ireland Act 1974

Criminal Justice (Confiscation) (Northern Ireland) Order 1990 [S.I. 1990/2588 (NI 17)]

Criminal Justice (Confiscation) (Northern Ireland) Order 1993 [S.I. 1993/3146 (NI 13)]

Proceeds of Crime (Northern Ireland) Order 1996 [S.I. 1996/1299]

Orders under Article 27 of the Criminal Justice (Confiscation) (Northern Ireland) Order 1990 (enforcement of external confiscation orders)

Criminal Justice (Confiscation) (Designated Countries and Territories) (Northern Ireland) Order 1991 [S.R. 1991/221]

Ditto, Amendment Order 1992 [SR 1992/469]

Ditto, Amendment Order 1993 [SR 1993/358]

Ditto, Amendment Order 1994 [SR 1994/164]

Ditto, Amendment (No.2) Order 1994 [SR 1994/350]

Criminal Justice (Confiscation) (Designated Countries and Territories) (Northern Ireland) Order 1992 [S.R. 1992/198]

Ditto, Amendment Order 1993 [SR 1993/359]

Ditto, Amendment Order 1994 [SR 1994/165]

Ditto, Amendment (No.2) Order 1994 [SR 1994/351]

Enforcement of external forfeiture orders

Criminal Justice (International Co-operation) Act 1990 (Enforcement of Overseas Forfeiture Orders) (Northern Ireland) Order 1991 [S.I. 1991/1464]

Note: this Order has been amended by the Orders listed in (a) above as amending England and Wales's Criminal Justice (International Co-operation) Act 1990 (Enforcement of Overseas Forfeiture Orders) Order 1991 [S.I. 1991/1463].

Rules of court

Supreme Court Rules

Order 116 of the Rules of the Supreme Court (Northern Ireland) 1980 [S.R. 1980/346]

Crown Court Rules

Crown Court Rules (Northern Ireland) 1979 [S.R. 1979/90]

Magistrates' Courts (Criminal Justice (International Co-operation) Act 1990) (No.2)
Rules (Northern Ireland) 1992 [S.R. 1992/191]

ANNEX B
Countries designated for drug trafficking confiscation and forfeiture co-operation which have ratified the 1988 United Nations Convention Against Illicit Traffic in Narcotic Drugs and Psychotropic Substances

Note: complete for England and Wales up to SI 1994/1640 and 1641 (Orders in Council covering drug proceeds and instrumentalities), which came into force on 1 August 1994. Co-operation in tracing, freezing and confiscating the proceeds and instruments of drug trafficking is possible with these countries:

2.	Afghanistan	Antigua and Barbuda
4.	Argentina	Armenia
6.	Australia	Azerbaijan
8.	Bahamas	Bahrain
10.	Bangladesh	Barbados
12.	Belarus	Bhutan
14.	Bolivia	Bosnia and Herzegovina
16.	Brazil	Brunei
18.	Bulgaria	Burkina Faso
20.	Burma	Burundi
22.	Cameroon	Canada
24.	Chile	China
26.	Colombia	Costa Rica
28.	Croatia	Cyprus
30.	Czech Republic	Denmark
32.	Dominica	Dominican Republic
34.	El Salvador	Ecuador
36.	Egypt	Fiji
38.	Finland	France
40.	Germany	Ghana
42.	Greece	Grenada
44.	Guatemala	Guinea
46.	Guyana	Honduras
48.	India	Iran
50.	Italy	Ivory Coast
52.	Japan	Jordan
54.	Kenya	Latvia
56.	Luxembourg	Macedonia, F.Y.R. of
58.	Madagascar	Malaysia
60.	Mauritania	Mexico
62.	Monaco	Morocco
64.	Nepal	Netherlands
66.	Nicaragua	Niger
68.	Nigeria	Oman
70.	Pakistan	Panama
72.	Paraguay	Peru
74.	Portugal	Qatar
76.	Romania	Russian Federation
78.	Saudi Arabia	Senegal
80.	Seychelles	Slovakia
82.	Slovenia	Spain

84.	Sri Lanka	Sudan
86.	Suriname	Sweden
88.	Syria	Togo
90.	Tunisia	Uganda
92.	Ukraine	United Arab Emirates
94.	United States	Venezuela
96.	Yugoslavia, F.R. of	Zambia
97.	Zimbabwe	

Additional countries which have ratified the Convention and in the process of designation by principal Order in Council under the Drug Trafficking Act 1994:

98.	Algeria	Belgium
100.	Belize	Cape Verde
102.	Chad	Cuba
104.	Ethiopia	Gambia
106.	Guinea-Bissau	Haiti
108.	Jamaica	Kyrgyzstan
110.	Lesotho	Malawi
112.	Mali	Malta
114.	Moldova	Norway
116.	Poland	Saint Kitts & Nevis
118.	Saint Lucia	Saint Vincent & Grndines
120.	Sao Tome & Principe	Sierra Leone
122.	Swaziland	Tajikistan
124.	Trinidad & Tobago	Turkey
126.	Turkmenistan	Uzbkistan
128.	Yemen	

ANNEX C:
Countries designated for Drug Trafficking and All Crime Confiscation and Forfeiture Co-operation which have ratified the 1990 Council of Europe Confiscation Convention

Note: complete for England and Wales up to SI 1994/1639, 1640 and 1641 which came into force on 1 August 1994. Co-operation in tracing, freezing and confiscating the proceeds of drug trafficking and other serious crime is possible with the countries listed below. (The Convention applies to Scotland on a drugs only basis, to be extended to all crime.)

Bulgaria	Finland
Italy	Netherlands
Switzerland	

Lithuania and Norway, which have also ratified the Convention, have been designated under the all crime legislation and are in the process of being designated for drug co-operation.

ANNEX D
Designated countries with which a Bilateral Confiscation Agreement is in force

Note: complete up to SI 1994/1640 and 1641, which came into force on 1 August 1994, and SI 1996/278. Co-operation in tracing, freezing and confiscating the proceeds of drug trafficking and other serious crime is possible with these countries:

A   DRUG TRAFFICKING AGREEMENT ONLY

	Country	*Date in force*
1.	United States	11.4.89
2.	Switzerland	21.6.90
3.	Australia	12.9.90
4.	Mexico	1.10.90
5.	The Bahamas	24.10.90
6.	Spain	15.12.90
7.	Saudi Arabia	20.9.91
8.	Bahrain	1.1.92
9.	Ecuador	1.3.93
10.	Barbados	1.6.93
11.	Colombia	25.11.93
12.	Uruguay	19.1.94
13.	Argentina	1.6.94
14.	Panama	1.9.94
15.	Malaysia	1.1.95
16.	Guyana	24.11.96

B   AGREEMENT COVERS DRUG TRAFFICKING AND OTHER SERIOUS CRIME

	Country or territory	*Date in force*
17.	Sweden	1.4.92
18.	Canada	17.9.93
19.	Nigeria	30.10.93
20.	Italy	8.5.94
21.	Netherlands	2.6.94
22.	India	1.5.95

C   AGREEMENT COVERS SERIOUS CRIME OTHER THAN DRUG TRAFFICKING

	Country	*Date in force*
23.	Mexico	1.8.96
24.	United States	2.12.96

ANNEX E
Published Multilateral Confiscation Conventions and Bilateral Confiscation Agreements

Conventions

(United Nations) Convention against Illicit Traffic in Narcotic Drugs and Psychotropic Substances, Opened for Signature at Vienna from 20 December 1988 until 28 February 1989 and subsequently at the United Nations Headquarters, New York until 20 December 1989, Presented to Parliament September 1989, Miscellaneous No. 14 (1989), Command 804, Treaty Series No.26 (1992), Command 1927.

(Council of Europe) Convention on Laundering, Search, Seizure and Confiscation of the Proceeds from Crime, Strasbourg, 8 November 1990, Presented to Parliament June 1991, Miscellaneous No. 10 (1991), Command 1561, Treaty Series No.59 (1993), Command 2337.

Bilateral agreements

Argentina
Agreement between the Government of the United Kingdom of Great Britain and Northern Ireland and the Government of the Argentine Republic concerning Mutual Judicial Assistance against Illicit Drug Trafficking, Buenos Aires, 27 August 1991, Presented to Parliament June 1994, Treaty Series No.31 (1994), Command 2592.

Australia
Treaty between the Government of the UK and the Government of Australia concerning the Investigation of Drug Trafficking and Confiscation of the Proceeds of Drug Trafficking, Canberra, 3 August 1988, Presented to Parliament November 1988, Australia No. 1 (1988), Command 503.

Bahamas
Agreement between the Government of the UK and the Government of the Bahamas concerning the Investigation of Drug Trafficking and Confiscation of the Proceeds of Drug Trafficking, Nassau, 28 June 1988, Presented to Parliament October 1988, Bahamas No. 1 (1988), Command 475, Treaty Series No.13 (1991), Command 1448.

Bahrain
Agreement between the Government of the UK and the Government of the State of Bahrain concerning Mutual Assistance in Relation to Drug Trafficking, Manama, 24 June 1990, Presented to Parliament November 1990, Bahrain No. 1 (1990), Command 1305, Treaty Series No.7 (1994), Command 2474.

Barbados
Agreement between the Government of the United Kingdom of Great Britain and Northern Ireland and the Government of Barbados concerning Mutual Assistance in Relation to Drug Trafficking, Bridgetown, 19 April 1991, Presented to Parliament June 1993, Treaty Series No.31 (1993), Command 2240.

Canada

Treaty between the Government of the UK and the Government of Canada on Mutual Assistance in Criminal Matters (Drug Trafficking), Ottawa, 22 June 1988, Presented to Parliament December 1990, Treaty Series No. 84 (1990), Command 1326. Note: now extended to all crime.

Ecuador

Agreement between the Government of the United Kingdom of Great Britain and Northern Ireland and the Government of the Republic of Ecuador concerning Mutual Assistance in Relation to Drug Trafficking, Quito, 7 May 1992, Presented to Parliament April 1993, Treaty Series No.18 (1993), Command 2162.

India

Agreement between the Government of the United Kingdom of Great Britain and Northern Ireland and the Government of the Republic of India concerning the Investigation and Prosecution of Crime and the Tracing, Restraint and Confiscation of the Proceeds and Instruments of Crime (including Crimes involving Currency Transfers) and Terrorist Funds, London, 22 September 1992, presented to Parliament September 1995, Treaty Series No. 69 (1995), Command 2957.

Italy

Agreement between the Government of the UK and the Government of the Italian Republic concerning Mutual Assistance in Relation to Traffic in Narcotic Drugs or Psychotropic Substances and the Restraint and Confiscation of the Proceeds of Crime, Rome, 16 May 1990, Presented to Parliament January 1991, Italy No. 1 (1991), Command 1395, Treaty Series No.33 (1995), Command 2853.

Malaysia

Agreement between the Government of the UK and the Government of Malaysia on Mutual Assistance in relation to Drug Trafficking, Kuala Lumpur, 17 October 1989, Presented to Parliament August 1990, Malaysia No. 1 (1990), Command 1176, Treaty Series No.42 (1995), Command 2883.

Mexico

Agreement between the Government of the UK and the Government of the United Mexican States concerning Mutual Assistance in Relation to Drug Trafficking, London, 29 January 1990, Presented to Parliament September 1991, Treaty Series No. 57 (1991), Command 1638.

Netherlands

Agreement between the Government of the United Kingdom of Great Britain and Northern Ireland and the Government of the Kingdom of the Netherlands to Supplement and Facilitate the Operation of the Convention of the Council of Europe on Laundering, Search, Seizure and Confiscation of the Proceeds from Crime, Strasbourg, 8 November 1990, presented to Parliament September 1994, Treaty Series No.45 (1994), Command 2655.

Nigeria

Agreement between the Government of the UK and the Government of the Federal Republic of Nigeria concerning the Investigation and Prosecution of Crime and the Confiscation of the Proceeds of Crime, London, 18 September 1989, Presented to Parliament December 1989, Nigeria No. 1 (1989), Command 901, Treaty Series No.18 (1994), Command 2447.

Panama

Agreement between the Government of the United Kingdom of Great Britain and Northern Ireland and the Government of the Republic of Panama concerning Mutual Legal Assistance relating to Drug Trafficking, signed Panama City, 1 March 1993, presented to Parliament October 1994, Treaty Series No. 46 (1994), Command 2660.

Saudi Arabia

Agreement between the Government of the UK and the Government of the Kingdom of Saudi Arabia concerning the Investigation of Drug Trafficking and Confiscation of the Proceeds of Drug Trafficking, Jeddah, 2 June 1990, Presented to Parliament November 1990, Saudi Arabia No. 1 (1990), Command 1308, Treaty Series No.65 (1992), Command 2097.

Spain

Agreement between the UK and the Kingdom of Spain concerning the Prevention and Suppression of Drug Trafficking and the Misuse of Drugs, Madrid, 26 June 1989, Presented to Parliament October 1989, Spain No. 1 (1989), Command 830, Treaty Series No.44 (1991), Command 1614.

Sweden

Agreement between the Government of the UK and the Government of the Kingdom of Sweden concerning the Restraint and Confiscation of the Proceeds of Crime, Stockholm, 14 December 1989, Presented to Parliament November 1990, Sweden No. 1 (1990), Command 1307, Treaty Series No.72 (1992), Command 2079.

United States of America

Agreement between the Government of the United Kingdom of Great Britain and Northern Ireland and the Government of the United States of America concerning the Investigation of Drug Trafficking Offences and the Seizure and Forfeiture of Proceeds and Instrumentalities of Drug Trafficking, London, 9 February 1988, Presented to Parliament March 1988, United States No. 2 (1988), Command 340, Treaty Series No.32 (1989), Command 755.

Uruguay

Agreement on Legal Assistance in relation to Drug Trafficking between the Government of the United Kingdom of Great Britain and Northern Ireland and the Government of the Oriental Republic of Uruguay, Montevideo, 23 January 1992, Presented to Parliament February 1994, Treaty Series No.4 (1994), Command 2458.